# LOVE NEVER DIES

89-WILL

# LOVE NEVER DIES

*Working Throught Grief to
Contact Your Mate
Who Has Passed Over*

# Joan T. Williams

| Library of Congres Number | 98-86690 |
| --- | --- |
| ISBN    (Hardcover) | 0-7388-0067-8 |
| (Softcover) | 0-7388-0068-6 |

This book was printed in the United States of America.

To order additional copies of this book, contact:
Xlibris Corporation
1-888-7-XLIBRIS
www.Xlibris.com

# CONTENTS

TO DOYLE,
AND TO BILL AND MARY,
WITHOUT WHOM THIS BOOK
MIGHT NEVER HAVE BEEN.

# CHAPTER 1

## THE DARKNESS

It stinks. The great, yawning void in life that used to be filled by a warm, loving, caring human being. It sometimes feels as if the world has come to an end. But somehow we stumble on; numb, looking back, and having to deal with situations that often we don't understand, can't cope with, and don't want to confront, anyway.

Well-meaning friends tell us that it is time to pull ourselves together and get on with life. We know that. The trouble is finding the energy and motivation to do it.

The fortunate, I believe, are those who have to earn a living after they have lost someone they love. I was one of those, and it certainly helped to have something to occupy my mind and a necessity to pay the bills.

My husband and I had been together for only sixteen years. We had met in the Persian Gulf where I was working as an executive secretary for an oil company, and he came out to drill an exploratory well.

It was a wonderful life. I lived in the company town, in company housing, along with all the other employees, with a houseboy to do the chores, a messing allowance, and a very adequate salary. Many of the bachelors didn't have a car, but there was always free transportation on company buses to go into town or down to the beach.

I had lived there for several years before Peter arrived and it wasn't long before his charm had captured my heart. But I was not one to plunge into matrimony at a minute's notice. I have to think about big decisions like that.

His job finished, Peter left the island and I went to work in North Africa, in Libya. Letters flew back and forth, and one day I packed my bags and headed for the States.

I was still uncertain about living in America, and I wanted to put my toe in the water, so to speak. All my life I have loved the ancient places of the world. I had puttered around ruins; plodded through the timeworn streets of Rome; wandered around Jerusalem, padding down the narrow alleys and drinking in the vibrations of times gone by. I had known the souks of Damascus, where stalls selling fabulous gold jewelry covered over half an acre. I had visited the Street Called Straight, where Paul was let down from a window in a basket to escape; and I loved Beirut, before the troubles, when it was an elegant and beautiful city and a shopper's paradise.

I had visited a friend of mine who lived in Sidon, Lebanon, where she took me to see a turkish delight factory down a narrow, cobbled alley where, in a dark cavern, a huge cauldron cooked the stiff, jelly confection, and it was packed into boxes at the entrance by three small boys, aged seven or eight. Like expert typists, their fingers worked independently from their eyes; they grabbed a pile of the cut squares of turkish delight from a large bowl, sprinkled .them with confectioner's sugar, and arranged them in layers separated by pieces of greaseproof paper in the wooden boxes stacked, with their lids, at their sides. Smiling, laughing, and chattering as they worked, just a few seconds sufficed to fill each box, competently and expertly. No machine could have been faster.

I had spent time in India, that vast, mystical continent. I had wandered around the Taj Mahal, the most beautiful monument to a dearly beloved wife; I had lived on a houseboat in Kashmir, and absorbed the beauties of the Gardens of Shalimar where flowers grow behind a tumbling waterfall.

I had climbed to the top of Crusader castles in Cyprus, set high on a mountain peak, and from the topmost level watched eagles planing below me.

I did not know how I would react to the newness of America.

It was, therefore, two years before we were married, but once settled in with Peter, I knew I had not made a mistake. This wonderful man surrounded me with love, caring, appreciation, and understanding.

Oh, there were differences about America. The way things always came in packaged multiples. I had to buy a packet of three wooden spoons, when all I needed was one.

Then there was the language barrier. I remember the time I wanted to buy Peter a flashlight for his birthday. So I went into a hardware store and asked, properly, I thought, for a torch.

The man in the store looked at me askance. "A torch?" he asked dubiously. "What are you going to use it for?"

What was I going to use it for? What kind of a dumb question was this? What does one usually use a light for?

"I wanted to put it in the car," I said, looking at him in amazement.

"Ah," he replied, light dawning. "You mean a flashlight." In England, no one but your great grandmother would call it a "flashlight." The man in the store was thinking "acetylene."

Then I was always getting into trouble with the parts of the car. What I knew as the bonnet was now to be called the hood. The boot turned into the trunk, mudguards were fenders.

A few years ago I went to visit my brother and his wife in England. Michael said there was a boot sale in the village hall and would I like to take a look? A boot sale? Well, I didn't really need a pair of boots, but I was willing to go along if he thought it might be interesting. When we arrived there were lots of small stalls selling anything and everything, rather like an outsized yard sale.

"Why do you call it a boot sale?" I asked him.

"Well," he explained, "it started with people parking in a field and selling stuff out of the boot of their cars." I realized I must now be thoroughly Americanized.

When it came to men's apparel, trousers were now pants, pants were now shorts, braces turned into suspenders, and suspenders became garters. When I went shopping I had to take a translator along.

"Closet," was another one. In England, a closet is a shortened form of "water closet," known colloquially in America as "the john." Now, here, the word meant a built-in space where you keep things, causing some misunderstandings.

Adjusting to a new land and a new culture is not always easy, but I flourished. How could I not, when I was loved so much? Every night, when we met after work, the first thing Peter said to me was, "And how was *your* day?" Not a word about his trials and troubles. He was kind. And not only to me, but to other people. A cruel, cutting remark that he overheard addressed to another, hurt him. He had the sensitivity to realize how the recipient felt.

We were living in Phoenix, Arizona, and at night we would stroll around the neighborhood, breathing in the heady, sweet scent of the orange blossom. He took so much pride in showing me the state. We visited the Grand Canyon and toured the small towns of Arizona. Peter pointed out the desert plants that we passed, the yucca, the saguaros, the mesquite, and once we even found a century plant in bloom. They are supposed to bloom after a hundred years and then they die.

As the years went by Peter's health began to fail. He had a heart attack. Things that had once been so easy for him now were a labor. But he never complained. It was only toward the end that he told me of the constant pain he suffered, and how, sometimes, at the end of the day's work in heavy construction, he would fiddle around with the car in the parking lot until all the others had left and then he would put his head down on the steering wheel and cry with the pain. Then he had to drive a hundred miles home.

He found a drink of liquor would help ease the constant pain and tightness in his chest, so he started drinking to keep himself going, and the more he drank, the more he damaged his heart and the more pain he had. It was a vicious circle.

Nobody can continue like this forever. Peter got weaker and

weaker but he wouldn't give up. And, like many men, he didn't want to take medication. He was forced into an early retirement.

Finally, there came a day when he said, "I guess I'd better go to the hospital." I made arrangements to take him in the next day. If he went to the hospital I felt he would get better. I was numb with worry and hope.

In the morning he could not stand. With great difficulty I managed to get him into the armchair in the bedroom. Slowly and painfully we struggled to get him into his clothes, the shorts, the shirt, and hardest of all, his pants. It took three hours. Then Peter absolutely insisted he was going to walk to the car. He suggested that I back it in so that the passenger side would be right by the back door. He struggled to his feet and immediately his knees buckled and he collapsed forward onto the carpet. He tried to crawl on his hands and knees but in a yard he could go no further and crouched on his knees with his arms and forehead on the floor.

Peter was too heavy for me to move. I ran outside to look for help. Most of the people who lived around us were either elderly or away at work. I tried next door but no one was in. As I came out onto the roadway I noticed a pickup stopped outside a house a few doors down on the other side of the street. A tall, burly, middle-aged man was standing by it. He was wearing khaki work clothes and I hurried across the road to him. I wanted to ask him for help, but he wasn't *that* young.

The first thing I blurted out was, "Excuse me, but do you have a bad back?"

He looked at me in astonishment—as well he might. "No," he replied guardedly.

"It's my husband," I explained. "I'm trying to get him into the hospital and he's collapsed. I wondered—" I got no further.

The man leaped forward. "Where is he?" he demanded.

"In the bedroom."

The man started towards the house he had seen me leaving. "No, no," I said. "I tried there, but there was no one in. It's next door."

He moved so fast I could hardly keep up with him. I let him into the bedroom. Peter had not moved.

"Is he injured in any way?" the man asked.

I shook my head. "No. He's just weak."

The man hoisted Peter into a sitting position on the bed and then hooked Peter's arm around his shoulders while his other arm was around Peter's waist, lifting him clear off the floor. The two of them started down the long hallway. Peter was smiling and his feet were moving back and forth in a walking motion. I followed.

"Thank you so much," I said to the burly, retreating back. "I couldn't have managed."

"Oh, he's doing most of it himself," my khaki-clad savior replied, with Peter's feet walking on air. And for the first time in my life I realized how important it is for a man to feel self-sufficient.

The man sat Peter in the car and disappeared. There was a small hiatus while Peter had to throw up. I was busy with bowl and paper towels when the man reappeared. "Are you all right?" he asked. "When I didn't see you leave I wondered if something was wrong."

I told him we would be all right and thanked him again. In a few minutes we were on our way to the hospital. He must have been an angel in disguise.

Arriving at the emergency room Peter was hustled into a wheelchair and engulfed in the hospital routine. After about half-an-hour a nurse arrived where I was waiting and handed me Peter's personal belongings. I walked into the room where he was still sitting in the wheelchair. His face was white and covered with sweat. "I guess they're going to keep me here for a while," he said bravely. I put my arms around him and kissed him and they wheeled him away.

That evening I was back at visiting hours. Peter was now in a room with another man. He was disappointed that his bed was not the one by the window but he smiled at me and said, "Maybe they'll change me over when the other fellow goes."

I was over at the hospital three times a day. Eleven o'clock was the earliest they would let me in and I stayed to try and coax Peter to eat lunch. He didn't want to eat; food didn't interest him. Then I rushed home to get something for myself and returned in the middle of the afternoon. Back home for a quick dinner, then I was at the hospital again in the evening until they threw me out at nine o'clock.

The first few days were taken up with tests and doctors probing and prodding and nurses running back and forth. Nobody would tell me what was going on; I could get no information from anybody. Finally, I phoned my own doctor and asked him if he could find out something. Perhaps they would talk to him if they wouldn't talk to me. I wanted to know. I had to know. He was my husband.

In a couple of hours my doctor phoned me back. There was little hope, he said, they were going to do what they could, but I was not to get my hopes high. The next day the doctor at the hospital took the time to talk to me.

"There is little we can do," he said brusquely. "If your husband lives he will be almost a vegetable. All he can look forward to is a life sitting in a chair, especially at his age." It sounded as though "his age" meant it was time for the scrap heap. He wasn't worth saving.

I had known for some years that one day this would happen, but when it actually hit I was shattered. What hurt me most was that the doctor had told me this in the hospital room, standing by Peter's bed. Peter must have been able to hear him for his voice was loud and calculated to carry. Perhaps he thought that if Peter had no hope he would just give up and die and save them the trouble of keeping him alive with IV's and tubes going in and out everywhere.

The doctor left and I walked out of the hospital room and down the corridor. I was crying. A man who had been visiting his old father in the bed next to Peter's followed me. He had heard. Now he put his arm around my shoulder as we walked together.

"He shouldn't have said that in front of him," he told me. "I know what you're feeling like. I lost my little girl a couple of years ago."

"I love him so much," I sobbed. "I can't bear to think of life without him."

"I know," the stranger replied. "But you wouldn't want him to go on living like that, would you?"

I shook my head. "He would hate it. He's always been so active."

We walked in the hospital corridor until I had stopped crying and dried my eyes. Then I could face Peter again. He never gave any sign that he had heard what the doctor said, but I knew he must have.

A day or two later Peter was taken to another hospital for some other tests, something to do with nuclear medicine. He now had a different doctor looking after him, an Indian lady who was very kind and so different from the first physician. Peter came back from these tests with lines and numbers written on his front. When I told him, he wanted to see, but he couldn't sit up, so I had to hold the small mirror from my handbag over his body while trying to get it at the right angle to satisfy his curiosity.

Two days later, the Indian doctor, Dr. Sheta, called me aside. She was pregnant and was wearing one of those smocks that had "Baby" and a down-pointing arrow on the front.

"I need to talk to you," she said gently. "There is really nothing more we can do. It's just a case of waiting for the end." She paused, then went on quietly, "I have to know whether you want us to take heroic measures to keep him going."

I thought of the needles and tubes Peter was now suffering so patiently. I shook my head. "No. If it's his time to go, let him go."

"Very well." She put her hand on my arm in a gesture of sympathy. "Don't cry," she said.

I knew then that it would not be very long. It wasn't.

The next morning I remembered how, several months before, one time I was leaving for the market, Peter had said, "Don't be too long. I don't want it to happen while you're away." I prayed now that he would still be alive when I got to the hospital and that it would not happen "while I was away."

When I arrived in Peter's room later that morning he was in a coma. His breathing was heavy and every now and then he gave a low moan. His eyes were half closed. I had never seen anybody in a coma before, but somehow I knew. A little nurse probationer came into the room.

"Do you want me to wake him for you?" she chirped.

"No, honey," I said. "He's not going to wake anymore."

I sat holding Peter's hand and stroking it. "I love you, Peter. I love you," I told him over and over again.

Saliva started to slip from the corner of his mouth. I wiped it away. His breathing became more and more shallow. Sometimes there would be a long pause and then he would draw another breath. Another nurse put her head around the door. I sat and waited.

Soon Dr. Sheta arrived. She took one look at Peter, put her arm around my shoulders and asked me to wait outside while she checked him. In a few moments she reappeared. She knew that I knew. "You can go in now," was all she said.

I returned to the room. The sheets had been straightened, pulled taut across his chest. The tubes and needles were removed. Peter's lower jaw had dropped and his mouth was open. His eyes had been closed.

Tears welled in my eyes. "Wait for me," I said in my heart. "Wait for me. But I don't want to hold you up in whatever you're going to do. But, if you can, please wait for me." Maybe he heard my thoughts. I didn't know.

I went home. A package was waiting in the mail box.

It was a book I had ordered for Peter. Several weeks before he went to the hospital, we had been watching TV one evening and something came up about a book called "De Re Metallica" by Georgius Agricola. "Oooh," said Peter excitedly, "I've always wanted that book." Peter had loved working in metal.

I hadn't really been paying much attention to the program,

but the name stuck in my mind, and the next day I started a hunt for it in the local bookstores. I thought it would be good to give Peter for Christmas. I finally discovered somebody who was familiar with it and said they would order it for me. Now it had arrived.

I sat in the living room and sobbed my heart out. No more will I reach over in bed and touch him. No more will I turn from the dressing table and see him lying there. No more will I hear him say, "Aren't you ever coming to bed?" No more will he give Bobbie, our cat, an upside-down cuddle. No more will he be making models. No more will he creep up behind me, give me a kiss on the nape of the neck and say, "Did you know I was in love with you?"

Peter had died the day before Thanksgiving, so it wasn't until the Friday that a friend came with me to the funeral home to make arrangements, and it was Friday evening that the minister who was to conduct the service came to visit me. He questioned me about Peter and we talked for a long time.

Peter and I had been married in a chapel under the auspices of the Church of Religious Science, and as we had no regular church affiliation, I asked for a minister from that church to conduct the funeral services.

The funeral was scheduled for the following Monday, and the funeral chapel held a small gathering of our friends. The minister finished his address with the words that I had told him Peter had said to me so often: "Whatever else happens to you in your life, know that you have been LOVED."

It was then that I cried.

The weeks following the funeral were a jumble of official things to do and the pain of sorting out my husband's things.

My brother came over from England for a week before Christmas, and it was a great help to talk to him. He and his wife had lost their little daughter seven years previously, run over outside their home, and he knew the pain I was going through.

My brother took back with him most of Peter's shirts and many of his tools and much of his drafting equipment. I also gave him Peter's cream leather jacket that had been a Christmas gift from me three or four years before. But when the day came for my brother to depart, the thought of that leather jacket going with him was too much to bear. Peter had been so pleased with it, with its many pockets, and he had looked so wonderful in it, that I became very quiet and withdrawn at breakfast.

Michael, my brother, is sensitive, too. "What's the matter?" he asked. "Have I done something?"

I shook my head. "I'm sorry," I said at last. "I know I said you could have that jacket, but it was Peter's favorite, and I really don't want to let it go."

My brother smiled. "Of course," he replied. "Perhaps you could have the sleeves shortened and wear it yourself."

I nodded. "Then it would feel as if Peter's arms were still around me."

Michael leaned across the breakfast table and kissed the top of my head. "You have given me a lot," he said. "You keep the jacket."

After I watched Michael's plane take off that night I felt more alone than ever.

The months that followed passed in a haze. There were days when I could do nothing but cry, off and on. At night I would reach out over the empty side of the bed and wail again.

For a year I marked the calendar with the number of weeks and the number of days since Peter had left me. Life was empty. I had no one but Bobbie, our cat, to care for. When I awoke in the mornings my first thought was, "Why should I get up? What is there to get up for?" One of my greatest difficulties was referring now to "my" and "mine," instead of "our." It just didn't seem possible.

There comes a time in everyone's life when he or she has to go on alone, in some circumstance or other. When we leave school and take our first job; when we leave home for the first time, perhaps for college.

Separation from those we love is hard to bear, but I know that if I had a choice I would not have wanted Peter to be lonely now as

I am lonely for him, and if one of us had to go first, then I am glad it was not me, for my wish and my love for him is only and all for his good and his happiness.

But we do not need to feel so alone. Our loved ones are there, willing, able, and even clamoring to help us, if we but reach out to them.

Helen Keller, that wonderful woman, once wrote:

> "We bereaved are not alone. We belong to
> the largest company in all the world - the
> company of those who have known suffering.
> When it seems that our sorrow is too great
> to be borne, let us think of the great family
> of the heavy-hearted into which our grief has
> given us entrance, and inevitably, we will feel
> about us their arms, their sympathy, their
> understanding."

This is true. But sometimes we need more, more than the feeling of sympathy from the untold millions who have trod this path before us. Whatever our beliefs on what happens after death, it would be of enormous help to feel and make contact with the one who is now missing from our life.

This is the story of how I accomplished that very thing. It made a tremendous difference in my living. It gave new hope and meaning to the small, everyday battles we wage constantly. It gave a feeling of warmth, of being loved and supported; the feeling that I was no longer struggling alone.

# CHAPTER 2

## IT'S SO HARD TO SAY GOODBYE

The months that followed the loss of my husband were hard to bear. Not only was I missing him, his jokes, his wonderful sense of humor, his love, but also the companionship I had come to depend on so very much.

I never thought this would happen to me. I had always been a loner. This was why I had been so hesitant to get married. It had to be somebody I could face over the breakfast table for the rest of my life, somebody I would feel comfortable with for years on end.

But Peter was just the man I had been looking for, how could I go on living without him? But I knew I had to— somehow. I have always thought that it is impossible to really understand the circumstances of another unless you have been there yourself. I know I had not understood the emptiness that follows the loss of someone you love, and I shuddered to think of the lack of sympathy I had shown at times. I hadn't understood, but now I did.

The first dinner I had alone at home after my brother left, I sat in Peter's place at the table, with my back to the bookcases, looking out into the room. I had made a small meat loaf, I remember, and had some greenies, as we used to call them, with it. Half way through I couldn't contain myself any longer and burst into tears. Was this what the next thirty years were going to be like? It seemed more lonely now than right after the funeral. Was it going to get worse instead of better?

I was desolate, and then I had the thought that Peter wasn't suffering anymore, the indignities of the hospital were over, no more struggling to get to the bathroom and sometimes failing.

I had said I loved him and wanted only the best for him, so I should not be despondent like this. If this was the best for him, then I must be brave and strong as he would have wanted me to be. It was easy to say, easy to tell myself, but so difficult to do. I laid my head down on the table and sobbed. I knew now why people went to seances and psychics, just longing to have some contact with the one they love, some touch, some feeling, something, anything.

But life has to go on. I struggled with work. I couldn't concentrate, couldn't spell. Time had no meaning for me, the days slipped by in a dim, dreary wasteland. All the things I had wanted to do while Peter had been so ill for so long were now meaningless because there was nobody to share them with. At night, in bed, I would stretch out my foot to the place where his had been, where we would touch, and there was nothing, emptiness, an emptiness that seared my soul.

Peter had wanted to be cremated and so, a few weeks after the funeral I went to the funeral home to choose an urn. A friend had urged me to put the urn in the cemetery, and had driven me out one day to look at the one where her husband was buried.

To me, accustomed to old English cemeteries, with trees, leaning gravestones, and flowers on the graves, this looked uninviting, like a field. Perhaps with the labor situation what it is, they are like that in England now, flat to facilitate the mowing.

Then my friend took me to the building to see the niches for a cremation urn. They reminded me of nesting holes for birds; some were so high it would have taken a tall ladder to climb up there. How could I put my Peter away in a bird's nest, high up in the wall.

I didn't know if I could afford one nearer the ground where it was more accessible. And besides, I would rather have the urn at home. Peter had loved his home, and if the urn were there, I would feel he was there with me, much more than if he were ten miles away hidden in a wall.

We stopped off at a McDonald's on the way home and my friend had a hamburger, but I was not hungry and just had a cup of coffee. I thanked her for showing me the cemetery, but privately felt I had already made up my mind to have my Peter in the house—our house—with me.

There were several urns to choose from at the funeral home, but many of them reminded me of jewelry boxes. Peter was a jewel but, no, I didn't really like them. Then the man at the funeral home brought out an urn that I fell in love with. It was urn-shaped, tall, with classical lines, and solid bronze. It was very heavy and much too tall to fit in a niche.

That made me decide. No niche. The bronze urn at home, sitting on Peter's chest of drawers. That was where it belonged. I bought it.

Then it had to be engraved. I decided on the wording, just his name and year of birth and death. I hoped I would be able to have Peter home for Christmas, but it was not to be. The engravers were swamped with work and could not even think about it until the middle of January. So be it. I had made my decision and that gave me some peace of mind. I felt Peter understood and approved.

Time went by, dragging its feet. I stumbled through work. Since I was working for myself as a legal transcriber, typing up court cases and depositions for court reporters, my time was pretty much my own, unless I had a rush job.

I found out I was earning about half of what I had been when Peter was alive. I just didn't want to get up in the morning (it used to be 5 a.m.) and therefore made a later start on the day. I couldn't concentrate. I wished I could just curl up into a little ball, not open my eyes, and let the day disappear. But I had to earn a living. There were some very small investments that we had, but nowhere enough to support me for more than a week or two.

Then Bobbie, our—no, now *my* cat, became ill. I took her down to the veterinarian's and came back with pills which she disliked taking. With no one to hold her while I popped them into her mouth, it wasn't easy. Another bane of widowhood. You have to do everything alone.

Bobbie got worse. She would not eat, drank very little and was always on and off her kitty sitty—a name Peter had given to the litter box. So, it was down to the vet's again. They tried some different antibiotic pills, but they achieved no better results.

In a couple of days I took her down for the third time. She was getting very dehydrated, and they suggested that they keep her for a couple of days and see if they could do something for her that way, force-feeding her.

I agreed. Then I remembered Peter and how he had been put through such trials at the hospital, force-feeding, needles, tubes, just like they wanted to do to Bobbie.

I told the veterinarian that I had just lost my husband after watching him die, inch by inch, for the last three years.

He asked, "How long is it since your husband died?"

"Three months," I answered. "And I don't want Bobbie to have to go through the same things that he did in the hospital as they tried to save him." I couldn't help it, a tear trickled down my cheek.

"Don't," he said. "I'm sure we'll be able to do something for her."

On the way out the receptionist gave me a couple of tissues and a cheering talk.

I phoned the vet the next day and he said Bobbie was "holding her own." It didn't sound very promising to me. However, the following day he phoned and said that I could bring Bobbie home. All the tests were negative and perhaps she would eat better with me than with them, for she still was not eating. So, I collected my little black sweetie and we came home. Bobbie still would not eat and kept throwing up the pill I gave her.

Again I phoned the vet. "She must have the medication," he said, "or the cystitis will return. Come down tomorrow and I'll give you some liquid for her."

I began to think I was not only going to lose my husband but my cat as well.

However, the liquid medicine seemed to work better or, at least, it was easier to get it into her, and gradually, over the next two weeks, she began to improve. Her fur became smooth again instead of spiky and she began to act more like her normal self.

I wish I could have said the same for me.

When I knew Peter was dying, many months before it actually happened, I had bought a book on dealing with being a widow. I knew that the loss of a spouse often triggers illness, and I made up my mind that I was not going to be ill. I couldn't afford it.

But I continued to be depressed and energyless. It seemed nothing could lift my spirits. Oh, I would put a good face on things—or try to—when around other people, but it was a mask that sometimes slipped. I was sitting with a friend one day, and something came up about Peter. My voice faltered and my eyes filled with tears.

"Oh, Joan," she said, sounding exasperated, "it's been three months!"

I didn't say anything, but I thought, "You don't know. You just don't know, as I didn't know before this happened." Daily I thanked God for the years we had together. Indeed, I am blessed that I received so much love and comfort and loyalty and support, so much caring and touching, so much welded togetherness. At the time it occasionally became irksome, but now that he is gone, I cherish the memory. We were, indeed, part of each other, and I am so lonely without him.

I am lonely for the sound of him puttering in his workshop, for the sight of him sitting across the table at mealtimes, for the little bits of information he would bring in from the outside world. I am lonely for the memories we shared, the reminiscences, the jokes.

Soon it was half a year and I didn't know where it had gone. I couldn't believe it had been so long; it seemed like yesterday that he was here.

And then I would remember how he was hurting and how he

continued working through the tremendous pain he never mentioned, simply to garner money for me, for he knew he was on the way out.

So it would have been selfish of me to wish him back in the condition he was. But I would look at old photographs and wish—oh, how I wished—that he could come back as he used to be, whole and healthy and alive, as he was before the arthritis in his spine, and his heart attack, and the liver trouble, for ever since these he had hurt in some fashion.

"Oh, Peter," I would think to myself so often, "wherever you are, I love you, and the ache in my heart is for you, only you.

"How can I count the years ahead, the empty, yearning years without you. One day I suppose it will lessen, the pain will start diminishing. But right now, you are still part of me, a very real part of me, deep inside. And half a year seems sometimes like a lifetime, and sometimes just a few hours. Time has lost its meaning and relevancy. It doesn't seem to exist anymore, not in the way it used to be."

I was so lonely for some sort of contact with Peter that two or three times I attempted to contact him using an Ouija board. But it wasn't any good. Nothing happened. That, too, was dead and still.

Several years before I came to the States, even, I was living and working in Benghazi, Libya, in North Africa. There I had been friendly with another English woman who one day mentioned quite casually that she and her mother and sister used to "play with the glass."

"Do you mean an upturned glass and a circle of letters?" I had asked.

"Yes."

"Well, I've heard about this—" I had tried to put it as delicately as possible— "and I wouldn't call anybody a liar, but sometimes people get a little carried away and their imagination expands. I'd really like to see this for myself."

"All right," she had replied, not in the least offended. "When we get back to the apartment, you can make some letters while I'm getting the dinner, and after dinner we'll have a go."

We did. She had been in charge at first, usually asking the questions because I was the novice. I could hardly believe what was happening. I had thought there would be cryptic words or odd letters that we would have to try to make sense of. None of it. It was just like having a conversation with a third person.

We were also told that this was a clumsy way of communicating. We should be still and we would get the answers directly in our mind. Oh, yeah! We stuck to the circle of letters.

We asked all sorts of questions and had received some very interesting answers. Everybody has a guide, and everybody has a path in life to follow. It is your guide's job to try and help you follow that path. It said, "Joan followed her path when she went to Bahrain."

This amazed me. For some years I had not been particularly happy living with my parents in England, but I had a beautiful home and many dearly loved books and possessions, and I like my comfort. The thought of leaving the countryside, living and working in the city all week, and only seeing my home at the weekend had not been appealing.

Finally, the English weather defeated me and I started looking for work in some sunnier climate. I applied for several jobs and the one that had come through first was the one in Bahrain, in the Persian Gulf.

Normally, I am stupidly sentimental about places, especially those I am leaving, but the day I left for Bahrain on a two-year contract, I walked out of my home and left my treasures without a backward glance or a stab of regret. It just "felt right." I might have been going to the mall for an afternoon's shopping. I was "following my path."

Time passed in Libya and my friend and I parted company; she went to West Africa and I to the States to be with Peter.

Occasionally, during the years we were married, I had used the Ouija board when Peter was working. He did not exactly look with favor on these proceedings. I think he thought I was a little weird. The board worked well for me and I used to have long conversations with someone.

One evening, right out of the blue, the board had spelled out, "Your husband is my son." Really! Peter had lost his father when he was twelve due to an accident at work. We had a long, animated conversation about my husband.

Several weeks later we were going to visit my mother-in-law on the coast. It was Mother's Day and there was going to be a small, family gathering, including Peter's sister, Marjorie. We were going to leave the following morning when my husband returned from the graveyard shift, and that evening I kept feeling an urge to get out the board, but had resisted it because I was busy. Finally, I got into bed and placed the board on my knee. The little, plastic cup I used started moving straight away.

"I would like you to give Marjorie a message from me," it spelled. "Can you do that?"

"Of course."

"It won't embarrass you, will it?" the board queried.

"Oh, no, not at all. Let me get a pencil and paper. All right. What's the message?"

"Tell her I want to come and visit her."

"Okay. Does she have to do anything special?" I had asked.

"Tell her to lie on her bed and think of my name."

"Fine." I wrote. A thought struck me. "By the way, what is your name?"

"Edward," the board spelled.

The next day when we arrived at Mother-in-law's house, I told Marjorie of the message. I said, "Your father wants to come and visit you." She didn't turn a hair. "He said he wants you to lie on your bed and think of his name."

Marjorie had nodded. "Okay."

"By the way," I added, "what was your father's name?"

"Marion."

My beautiful bubble burst. "Oh," I said, oozing disappointment, "he said his name was Edward."

"Oh, that's Grandfather Williams," Marjorie replied, matter-of-factly.

Peter's grandfather had idolized him, and when he was small used to take him on his cattle-buying trips in his private railroad coach during the summer holiday. He would take Peter downtown on business meetings and introduce this five-year-old to local businessmen who solemnly shook his hand.

My husband, of course, never called his grandfather by name, but always referred to him as "Grandfather," and I had never inquired as to his given name. I suppose the word "son" was used in a loose connotation.

But now, with Peter gone, my Ouija board techniques seemed useless. I felt very low. I missed Peter so much that at times it was unbearable. There was one thing, however, that sustained me.

When the doctor, Dr. Sheta, had told me that Peter was dying, I was desolate. I had come home and prayed that Peter would have an easy passage and that I would be there with him when he went. And I was.

When Peter was in a coma and I was telling him, "Peter, I love you. I love you," he gave no sign that he could hear me. But I remembered something that had happened one day during one of my visits to the hospital.

A male nurse was taking blood samples from my husband, who lay silent and unmoving in the bed while the nurse talked to him.

"Do you think he can hear you?" asked one of the visitors to the patient in the next bed.

"Certainly," answered the nurse. "He can hear. Even in a coma, hearing is the last sense they lose."

This sustained me after Peter died. The thought that perhaps he could hear me, even if he gave no sign; the hope that he knew I was there with him, as he had wanted it to be. But how could I be sure? Perhaps comas were different for different people. How did the nurse know?

The day after Peter died was Thanksgiving. I refused all the well-meant, kind invitations to join a Thanksgiving gathering in the home of my friends. I could not face it, remembering the holiday dinners Peter and I had shared. The time I cooked the turkey   •
upside down until he pointed out that it looked peculiar. I wanted to be alone at Thanksgiving with my grief and my memories.

Then I noticed the time. I walked slowly into our bedroom. I knelt by the bed and stretched my hands over the cover, in imagination holding his hands as I had done the day before at the hospital. The clock ticked on until 1:27 p.m., the time his spirit had finally slipped from the battered body.

I felt a great peace envelop me. I raised my head. "Peter," I said out loud, "if you could hear me yesterday, if you knew I was there with you, please bring back your little magnets."

My husband was an engineer. For many years he had worked as a driller and then as an operating engineer in heavy construction, usually on a crane. But at heart he was an inventor. No sooner presented with a problem but his brain busied itself with a solution. He designed a new type of oil drilling rig, able to drill at an angle direct from the surface, instead of whipstocking, as it is called, branching out at an angle from a vertical shaft underground. He solved a problem in the manufacture of titanium - just as the demand for it dropped, unfortunately. He developed a sun tracker for a solar energy device to keep the unit centered on the sun.

And for all his inventions he made working models. Wheels turned, lights flickered, tiny electric motors hummed. When he wasn't inventing, he made models from the past. He begged my two round egg poacher pans, which were just what he needed for the boiler on his model of Cugnot's steam car.

Peter never used kits for his models. He picked up bits and pieces, like my egg poacher pans, when and where he came across them. And every day he carried those two small bar magnets with him in his watch pocket to test if the things he bought or found were steel. They were as much a part of him as his comb or his reading glasses.

When they were not in his pocket, his two little magnets clung to the nightstand, a three-tier metal serving cart and a left-over, useful economy from the time when we first bought the house.

A few days after Peter had gone into the hospital, I noticed the magnets were missing from their accustomed perch on the front edge of the nightstand. For some reason it bothered me. Down on my knees I combed square yards of shag carpet with my fingers; I peered under the top shelf to see whether, still clinging to the metal, they had somehow been pushed up underneath; I craned my neck to peek under all the corners. They were nowhere to be found.

Peter had gone into the hospital with his pockets stuffed with wallet, car keys, money, credit cards, pens and pencils, all of which the hospital had returned to me, along with his shirt, when they admitted him. Perhaps, I thought, he had taken his magnets with him, too.

I scoured the closet in his hospital room where nurses had hung his pants, but there were no magnets. Pants on a hanger quickly shed their pocket contents as any man (and many a wife) knows, and I presumed that somewhere between the emergency room where he had been admitted, and the bed in which he lay, his little magnets had been lost.

Now, I rose from my knees at the side of our bed. Thanksgiving Day. Even through my grief I could truly give thanks for the wonderful husband who had shared my life for sixteen years, for the love he had given me, the gentleness he had shown me.

I felt convinced that some day, somewhere, I would find his two little magnets, perhaps at the back of a drawer, perhaps in a jar with other things among nails or screws, or simply among the clutter on his workbench.

The Saturday afternoon following Thanksgiving I was lying on the bed, reading. I glanced over toward Peter's side of the bed, as I had done so many times during the two weeks he was in the hospital. My gaze wandered on to the nightstand with his watch, his reading glasses, alarm clock, medicine bottles, pencils.

There was a dirty mark on the inside curve of the nightstand's metal leg, the front left-hand one, about two inches down from the top shelf. Curious as to what could have caused it, I rolled off the bed and went around to the other side. Once more I bent down and peered under the top shelf.

There, nestled neatly together, spanning the inside of the leg, were Peter's two little magnets.

Peter had known I was there with him at the hospital when his spirit slipped from his worn-out body into the "new and more elegant edition, revised and corrected by the Author," as envisaged by Ben Franklin.

My heart soared. He had known. He was around somewhere. "Oh, Peter, Peter, talk to me. Let me know your presence; let me feel you around me in the house, somewhere, everywhere."

From time to time during the months following I would come into a room of the house and find it flooded with a beautiful perfume, usually the smell of roses. Peter had loved roses. Was it my husband sending these beautiful scents?

Several months later I joined a yoga class. One evening, as we were lying stretched out on the floor with closed eyes for the final fifteen minutes of relaxation and visualization, the instructor lit some incense. I love incense, and I relaxed even more as the perfume wafted over me. When we arose I asked the instructor what was that beautiful incense he had lit.

"I didn't light any incense," he said. "What are you talking about?"

"But I smelled it. Didn't you smell it?" I asked, turning to the rest of the class. They all shook their heads. I was baffled until I remembered the rose scents I had experienced at home. It must have been Peter, I thought. If you can send the scent of roses, I don't suppose it's any more difficult to do the same with incense.

But beautiful though these scents were—and I felt sure it was Peter's doing—I wanted more. I felt frustrated until ten years later I met two new friends, Bill and Mary.

They helped change my life.

# CHAPTER 3

## THE BREAKTHROUGH

Bill and Mary came into my life when I started attending evening classes in astrology in which I have always been interested, and we soon became good friends. One day I was telling Bill about my experiences with the circle of letters and the upturned glass when I was living in North Africa. As I had done, he said, "Well, I'd really like to see this for myself."

"Okay. Why don't you and Mary come over one night next week, then," I said, "and we'll set it up and try."

So, a week or two later Bill and Mary came over for the evening.

We set up a circle of letters and a small, plastic medicine cup. It started moving almost immediately, but we had little success with getting answers other than "Yes" and "No.' Bill and Mary had come over with several questions they wished to ask, but there seemed to be little response. I was disappointed. This had worked so well in North Africa and I felt I had rather let them down. Perhaps they thought my imagination was soaring, too.

Suddenly, Bill said, "Joan, this evening is for you."

"For me?" I didn't have any questions.

Then Bill, who is very sensitive, asked if I ever lit the candles which were in a four-candle holder on the table.

"Not since Peter died," I said. "We used to have dinner by candlelight every night. They have sat here for the past eleven years unlit. I couldn't bear to light them after our last dinner to-gether."

"Would you mind if they were lit now?" Bill asked.

"No, that's fine," I replied, and went in search of matches. We lit the candles and there was a different atmosphere in the room immediately.

A faint smell of cigarette smoke wafted through the room. After a minute or two it became stronger. The little cup started swinging back and forth between the letters C and R.

Bill and Mary had never known Peter, and I hadn't talked to them about him. C and R. What was this about? Bill and Mary shook their heads. They couldn't figure that it was anything to do with them. Besides, Bill had said this evening was for me. C and R. didn't mean anything to me.

Bill asked, "Did Peter smoke?"

I nodded. "Like a chimney. He always said he would time things with a cigarette, but he only got through a carton a week, so I suppose that's not as bad as it could have been."

The cup continued swinging from C to R and back again. The scent of smoke was replaced by that of roses. We sat with our fingers lightly on the upturned cup while it swung strongly.

Bill said, "The person here is your guide. Do you know the name of your guide?"

I shook my head.

Bill said, "It's Peter. He's here."

My heart leapt. "Peter? Is that really you?"

The cup went to "Yes." Then slowly and hesitantly it spelled out "Candles."

I was speechless. My Peter! Here! I felt tears of joy prickle the back of my eyes. I asked, "Are you happy?"

"Yes."

"Are you busy?"

"Yes."

Bill asked, "What are you doing now?

The cup wavered and hesitated. Bill's sensitivity came through for him. "Was Peter in the Service?" he asked me.

"Yes," I answered. "In the army. World War II."

"He finds it difficult to move the cup," Bill said. Then he

added, "Are you helping soldiers now?"

The cup went to "Yes."

"From World War II?" asked Bill.

The cup went to "No."

"Vietnam?"

The cup slid to "Yes."

"You are helping soldiers from Vietnam?" I asked.

Again the cup said "Yes."

Peter had seen a lot of grief during World War II, in Europe. He had been in six invasions, none of them at H-Hour, but five of them on D-Day. He told me once that when he went into the army—and he had volunteered—he made up his mind that he could have no close friends, that it would be too painful if some-thing happened to them. Peter was very sensitive, despite his tough exterior, more sensitive than perhaps anyone but I knew.

I have never forgotten the time he told me about how, as the sergeant in charge of a patrol, he had discovered Dachau, one of the worst extermination camps. To this day, I can repeat every-thing he told me word for word. The horrors he saw during World War II never left him, and until we were married he used to have many nightmares.

Peter had fought at Monte Cassino, and he used to tell me of the mules coming down the mountain, every night, and across the back of every mule was the body of a dead soldier. When he told me he cried. It was no wonder to me that he was now helping other soldiers. He knew. He understood.

The scent of roses was still with us. Bill said, "Peter has a new name now. When they get there they have a new name.

"Can you tell us your new name?" he asked.

The cup swung from C to R.

"So, CR is your new name?" I queried.

"Yes," went the cup.

Bill said, "CR sends you a rose."

My heart sang. A few months after Peter died I was going through his things, and tucked away in his camera case I found a small clipping from the newspaper. It was a poem. Before I arrived in the States, Peter would occasionally clip one of these poems that appeared daily and include it in his letter. This one started:

"Do not weep for me, beloved,
"When my time has come to die..."

and one of the lines further on said,

"And my heart with scarlet roses
"In your garden shall appear."

I had treasured that little clipping. It was from the days when he was living in Phoenix and he must have clipped it sixteen or seventeen years before he died. The whole poem was beautiful and I had fashioned a melody for it and used to sing it to myself day after day. I did have a scarlet rose in the garden, and every time I passed it, even when it was not in bloom, I thought of Peter. And now he was sending me a rose!

"Does it help to light the candles?" I asked.

"Yes," went the cup.

I remembered something from past experiences. "If I sit quietly, will you come into my mind?"

The cup slid to "Yes."

"All I have to do is sit quietly and think of CR, your new name, and you will come to me?" I asked.

"Yes," went the cup.

When Bill and Mary had left I sat in the armchair with the smell of the candlewax still strong in the room and thought of CR. He came immediately and we talked. I don't remember about what; all that mattered was just being near to him. It was a sort of holding hands.

I remembered all the times we had sat in companionable silence; the times we had ridden in the car, simply enjoying the scenery; the little jokes we had shared. I could now look at photos of Peter and realize that he was right there, with me, as soon as I thought of his new name. He would come whenever I reached out for him. My happiness was overflowing.

After that, in the evenings, I would sit down at the dining room table, light the candles, and with pencil and paper try to capture some of the conversations we had. I don't write very fast, and the resulting scribbles were almost indecipherable.

About two weeks later I had an idea. If I typed out the questions during the day, then in the evening I would only have to scribble in the answers. No sooner thought than done. I sat down at the typewriter, put paper in the machine and started: Q. I have some more questions about candles.

Suddenly there was a reply in my head. "Go ahead."

I sat with my mouth open. Then I recovered. I typed again: "Are you there, right now, as I am typing?"

"Yes. What is your question?"

I was so stunned I had forgotten my question. When I was using the Ouija board on my own during the evenings while Peter was working, it had often said that if I would be quiet and still the answers would come into my mind.

"I would think I was putting the answer there myself, then," I had objected.

"No," the board spelled, "you will know the difference."

But I had been too afraid of deceiving myself and making up the answer I wanted to hear, to believe that this was possible. Now it had happened I *did* know the difference.

"This is fun," I typed. "Is it any more difficult for you to do it this way?"

"Not really," came the answer.

So, from then on, every day I sat down at the typewriter and typed questions and answers. I set up a single white candle by the typewriter, lit it, relaxed, thought of CR, and started my questions. At first I typed on an ordinary piece of paper and then, later transferred it into the looseleaf book I was keeping as a record of these contacts. After three or four days, however, this seemed too much of a double labor, and I gained enough confidence to type directly into my record book. This I have done ever since.

Each evening, when I sat down at the typewriter, a host of questions flooded my mind. I asked about anything and everything, hopping from subject to subject.

I asked, "How can I enhance my ability to be more aware of your presence?"

"Relax more," CR replied. "Meditate. Don't be so busy-minded when you are doing nothing."

I had recently had a severe attack of shingles and the pain was still lingering. I asked how could I eliminate the pain?

"Be more loving," came the answer.

"To whom?"

"To your mother, for one," CR said. "Do not continually go over the troubles between you."

At every session I told Peter, or CR as I now called him, that I loved him, and he replied in the same way. I asked if anything made a difference to this contact, the time of day, the phases of the moon, the color clothing I wore, things like that.

"These things don't make a difference," he answered, "but what does make a difference is regular meditation. It helps to still the mind and makes you more receptive."

I was so happy now that I had Peter back to talk to, even if I could not reach out and physically touch him. I looked back one day at a journal entry I had made six months after Peter had died. It went:

> "I HATE TUESDAYS. I hate them worse
> than Wednesdays, the day Peter went into
> the hospital and the day he died.
> Tuesday is the last day he was at
> home; the last night we spent together;
> the last day he said meaningful things
> to me; the last day in the hospital
> that he talked to me.

"I am so angry on Tuesdays that I
feel I would like to go out and kill
somebody just to relieve the tension,
the bitterness of being left here while
Peter is gone.

"I hate Tuesdays."

I didn't feel that way anymore. We talked. He was always there whenever I thought of his new name. We held the sort of inconsequential conversations that people do, only this time one was in a body and one wasn't.

Once I said, "Do you remember the time we went to California for three days and it came out later that you wanted to see it for the last time, you said?"

"Yes, I remember," CR replied.

"Can you see California now, from where you are?"

"Yes."

"Can you see anywhere?"

"Yes."

"I thought at the time you said that, many years ago, that when you had left the body you would still be able to see California, and I wanted to tell you, but I didn't know whether you would accept it."

"I might not have admitted it then," CR answered.

I switched my thoughts again. "You brought back your little magnets," I reminded him. "I thought that, perhaps, having been so ill for so long, you would have to spend some time recuperating, as it were, before you could do things like produce the scent of roses and bring back your magnets."

"Not really."

"Don't people who have been ill a long time have to spend some time recuperating there, at first?"

"Not usually," CR replied. "In some extreme cases, maybe, but not as a rule."

I had been doing some artwork for a client and CR remarked

on it. "I liked your little house."

"Thank you," I said. "It was fun to do."

"You are getting to be fairly good," CR went on. "You will get much better. Just practice."

"If you could arrange for me to win a bunch of money," I suggested, "then I wouldn't have to spend so much time working, and I could practice more."

"I'm not allowed to do that."

"Not allowed?"

"We have rules here as well, you know."

"Can you tell me some of your rules?" I asked.

"We are not allowed to hurt people, nor are we allowed to help them. You have to struggle and make it on your own. We are allowed to present opportunities, but it is up to you, on the earth plane, to make the most of them. If you don't progress and make the most of your opportunities, then we cannot do more for you. It is up to you, each individual."

"A long time ago, in North Africa, we were told that it is our guide's job to try and help us follow our spiritual path. What are you trying to help me do now?"

"Lots of things," CR replied. "Meditate, for one. Read more, for another. Relax and stop worrying about every little minute."

"I see. I'll try and do better."

"All lessons have to be learned on earth," CR added.

"Is it possible to learn lessons over there?"

"Not the lessons you are supposed to learn on earth."

"Such as?" I prompted.

"Be good to others. Do to them as you would have them do to you. Be compassionate and helpful."

"What sort of lessons do you learn where you are? I asked.

"I can't tell you," CR said.

"Is there a learning process or do you just do certain work for which you are fitted?"

"Oh, yes, we learn; we attend classes, particularly at first."

"Do you have training for the work that you do?"

"Oh, yes, we are trained."

"It must make you feel good to be helping people who need it, or presenting opportunities, rather," I said.

"Yes, it does," CR came back. "But it isn't always easy here, as on earth, to get them to accept it."

"That must be frustrating."

"Yes, it is, but we are taught to be patient."

During the days, when I was not busy, or after the evening's session on the typewriter finished, I would read through my typewritten pages over and over again. They comforted me. They encouraged me to know that Peter was still around and still caring for me and about me.

Whenever I talked to him I didn't call him "Peter" anymore, but "CR." But whatever the name, I knew it was my Peter. I felt as close to him as I had when we were married and he was off for the day working. He didn't have to be in the house then for me to know that he loved me, and I knew now that he still loved me, even though he was not and never would be physically in the house again.

A couple of months after their first visit Bill and Mary again joined me for an evening's conversation, for questions in which they were interested. This time, however, we used the typewriter.

In the meantime, Bill had been receiving messages on his own. He asked if the word "S-C-I-O-R" meant anything.

"Yes," came the answer. "What do you want to know?"

"I want to know what is significant about that word," Bill responded.

"It is the transliteration of an ancient word from Babylon used by the priests when conducting ceremonies. It should be used in the present time with care, for it is a powerful word."

I chipped in, "Bill says this word came to him as being your name now, rather than the initials CR. You did say that was a phonetic rendering, didn't you?"

"Yes, I did," came the reply, "and yes, Bill is right. That would be the spelling of my name, but when I first came through to you with the letters and the little cup, it was difficult for me to communicate, and this seemed to be the easiest way to give you something to be able to pronounce. It is pronounced 'See-or.'"

"So, now we shall call you 'Scior,' is that right?" I asked.

"That is my name, yes, and now you have the spelling for it you might as well use it. Don't you think that would be a good idea? I would like it."

We all agreed. So, now my Peter turned from "CR" into "Scior."

My nightly sessions on the typewriter lengthened, sometimes into an hour and a half or more, and the questions became longer and the answers more complicated.

After a few months my questions began to thin out, and when Scior asked me if I had any questions, I would say, "No. I can't think of anything particular at the moment." It was then that he started giving what I can only characterize as lectures. Scior would say, "Tonight we will talk about such-and-such," and there would follow pages and pages of typescript on certain aspects of life and living, interspersed with questions from me on various points.

The only people who knew about these conversations were Bill and Mary. Mindful of Scior's admonition not to broadcast these things, I had told no one of what was happening. Bill, too, suggested that I keep quiet about it.

"You are still a little unsure," he said. "You are still wondering whether this is really true, and although you are convinced in your own mind that this is Peter, I think it would be wise not to have any negative input."

It was true. Most of me believed it was Peter, but there was a questioning portion of my mind that knew how easy it is to deceive oneself. I mentioned this from time to time to Scior, but he always reassured me that this was not my imagination running riot. So, after a few months, I told my best friend, Sylvia.

I was so happy that I had made contact with Peter, and I wanted to share my happiness.

I wished I hadn't.

# CHAPTER 4

## THE IMPORTANCE OF LOVE

Sylvia and I were having breakfast when I told her.

"You're not going to believe this," I started, "but I've made contact with Peter."

I babbled on, telling how all this had happened, how happy I felt, it was so wonderful to be able to talk to him again. I told her some of the exciting information he was giving me. Finally I shut up.

Sylvia never answered me. She changed the subject completely and started talking about something quite different.

I was crushed. I felt as though she had slammed a door in my face. I knew she thought I was making up all this, it was just a figment of my imagination. I was too hurt to try and sustain my position. Why bother, I felt, if a mind is closed, it usually remains that way. She is entitled to her opinion, as I am to mine. We continued a conversation on the subject she had brought up.

That night I talked to Scior about it.

"Sylvia is different from you," he said. "She has a more analytical mind, while you are intuitive. It takes time for some people to accept the things that are happening to you and the fact that we are having these conversations. Be patient."

"She hurt me," I complained. "Perhaps I am too sensitive. I have to learn to take these things in stride."

"It is not wise to share these kinds of things with people for a while, Joanie. This is new to you," Scior went on. "Do not be hurt.

Send her loving thoughts. This will erase the hurt, for she did not mean to hurt you."

"You have talked before about love," I said, "and loving thoughts. Could you tell me a little more?"

"Loving thoughts," Scior replied, "are one of the most important things you can do, both for yourself and for others, including those of us here.

"When you send a loving thought to someone, it surrounds them with a feeling of warmth and closeness, and it leaves behind, with you, the sender, the same feeling, although you may not notice it as much as the one who receives the loving thought.

"It is especially important," Scior went on, "for those of us over here."

"Can I help you now, from here, by loving you?"

"Indeed, you can."

"But I do love you and have always loved you, when you were with me and after you had gone."

"I know," Scior answered. "Love is the most important thing there is. And I'm not talking about sexual love, but love in its broadest sense."

"How can I love you more than I do?" I asked.

"By remembering the good things in our relationship; by thinking happy thoughts of me; and by keeping me in your heart. I know you can't do this when you are busy, but there are many moments when it would be a help if you could send me a loving thought, just for a moment. They are very precious."

"And they help? In what way?"

"They help me to do my job here and they will make us to be together longer."

"If people here want to help someone who is over there, is that what they have to do, send them loving thoughts?"

"Yes," Scior replied. "It is of tremendous help, more than you know. It makes a lot of difference to us here. That warm little glow that you project when you think of someone lovingly comes here like a great light."

"Thank you for telling me that, Scior."

"As I said," Scior went on, "loving thoughts help people on earth, too, when sent or received, although you probably do not feel it as strongly as we do here, where everything is mental.

"Every loving thought you send to anyone carries a message, and whether they are actively aware of it or not, it makes a difference. But to us here, it is a tremendous benefit."

"I will send you many loving thoughts from now on," I said, "more than before."

"Think of them as points of light."

"Points of light? That sounds like a political speech."

"Not at all," Scior responded. "It is far from being a political speech.

"When humans first come over here, the thing that strikes them most is the light. It makes everything seem clearer and more brilliant than are on earth. Compared with human eyes looking at the earth, humans see things covered with a sort of veil or fog, dimly, compared to what the same thing appears to us here.

"When we look at things, they sparkle and the colors are so very different from what you see in your human bodies. You may think that the colors of something are beautiful and brilliant, but compared to what we see, they are dull and misty."

"That sounds as though yours might be a little garish," I said.

"Not at all. It is just that the light is different. Do you know why it is different?"

"No. Tell me."

"Because of the loving thoughts that are sent our way," Scior replied.

"Some churches on earth pray for the souls of the dead, and although this is not a loving thought sent to an individual, it is something akin, a more collective effort, if you like to put it that way," he went on.

"Then, very often, people who have lost someone departed from the body will pray for them, think of them lovingly, remember them lovingly, and all these loving thoughts each create a small point of light. Collectively they make the light here very different from that on earth. They are vibrating at a different rate from earthly vibrations, and this intensifies and magnifies the brilliance."

"So, every time I looked at a photo of you and remembered you with love, that created a point of light?" I asked.

"Correct. And when you think of all the photos and mementos that people look at and think about, you can see how this comes about, this difference in the light."

"What happens if someone here thinks disparagingly of an entity over there? Does it extinguish a point of light?"

"No," Scior replied. "It does not affect the general atmosphere, only the individual entity."

"How does it affect the individual entity?"

"It causes them pain. And since nothing here is physical, it is all mental, it is a mental pain they feel. The nearest I can describe it so that you would recognize it, is to say it is something like sorrow or remorse that a human would experience, only in a very much more pronounced way.

"None of us was perfect when on earth," Scior continued, "but when we are reminded of our faults and failings while we were there, it is like a black cloud hanging over us. We see now all the things we did wrong—"

"As I will when I get there," I interrupted.

"—yes, that is true, and since we cannot do anything to rectify them now, it is a big burden to carry. If more people on earth knew how much it hurts to speak and think ill of those of us over here, I am sure they would not do it, however irritating we were while on earth."

"I won't do that anymore. I didn't realize it made such a difference."

"Oh, yes, indeed it does. We know that people still on earth don't realize how much it hurts, and perhaps it assuages their feelings of frustration and anger, which they either could not or would not express to us while we were with them, but nobody is perfect, Joanie, while on earth, nor are we here.

"We are all learning. The time will come when those newly come here will look back on their life and see whom they upset and how, and not be able to mend things or make amends for their stupidity or thoughtlessness, or whatever else irritated the ones they were with."

"There is an old saying, 'Don't speak ill of the dead,'" I said, "but I never realized it had such a practical application."

"Yes, Joanie, it does. So, try to put away the bad memories you have of us."

I thought for a moment. "It must be very difficult for the relatives of, say, a murdered human, to feel anything but bitter thoughts about the one who did it. Or someone killed by a drunken driver. Surely you cannot expect these people to think lovingly of the one who caused the death?"

"No," Scior replied. "We understand these very human reactions, and experiencing these reactions is something that the one who caused the death has to put up with. Previously, some churches referred to this state as purgatory, and believe me," Scior went on, "it is very uncomfortable for the entity involved."

"Does it ever improve?"

"Usually not for a very long time, for these bitter memories are difficult for a human to erase, and until the humans can bring themselves to truly forgive, the situation for the entity over here remains the same.

"When all the humans who harbor bitter thoughts about this incident are over here, only then can the entity who caused them begin to start growing here."

"So, a loving thought creates a point of light," I queried, "as well as being beneficial to the recipient?"

"Yes, Joanie, it does. It has a double effect. And the more loving thoughts an entity here receives, so the area around them becomes even brighter. They have what you might call an aura of points of light."

"Those entities that don't receive many loving thoughts, are they sort of darker?"

"Yes, Joanie, they are. It is always very sad for us to see them.

"We can always tell who is not receiving any or many loving thoughts. Many of them are humans who have drifted away from their families, who have died in obscurity with no one to mourn for them. These are the ones who benefit most from the prayers for the souls of the departed, but it is a sort of generic benefit, which is not nearly as beneficial as that from humans who remember us with loving thoughts."

I remembered how debilitated and distraught I had been in the months and years after Peter had died. How numb I had felt, how nothing in life had meaning.

"What about the people left behind on earth?" I asked. "How can we help ourselves to face the emptiness and the anguish that we feel after those we love have gone?"

"I know it is hard," Scior replied, "but the first thing to remember is that what humans call death is a natural thing; it happens to all living things at one time or another.

"The second thing to remember is that these loved ones are not gone forever. Those left behind will see them (if they wish to) when they, too, come over to this side.

"And remember that we, who have left the body, are probably nearer to you now than when we were on the earth plane. I know you cannot reach out and physically touch us, but there are other ways to reach us, as you have found, although it may take a little time and needs persistence."

"Is where you are Heaven, then?" I asked.

"I suppose you might call it that," Scior replied. "So many religions talk about 'Heaven' as if it were some far-away place that is so inaccessible to those still on earth, and the ones left behind find this depressing. But as you know, contact between those who love—and love can take many forms—can be achieved with the right attitude of mind, the right approach, and patience.

"If those who were left behind would remember this, I am sure it would help alleviate their natural grief.

"It is natural to grieve, and most necessary for a human. There has been a parting of the contacts; it is no longer possible to hold someone, be it child, parent, sibling, or lover, in your arms. There is a feeling that expressions of emotion fall on empty air and cannot be received by those they are aimed at and for."

I nodded my head in silent agreement. That was just how I had felt.

"This is not so," Scior went on. "We, over here, are keenly aware of the thoughts and emotions that those still on earth send us. We receive them, absorb them, and this should be borne in mind by those still on earth. Whether the thoughts are good or bad, we receive them and absorb them.

"It is no good railing at Fate and complaining that your husband or your mother has left you to cope with life alone. Life may be difficult when these supportive people are gone, but there are lessons to be learned by the ones left behind; lessons that will strengthen them and enable them to progress better through life than if they were supported by another all the time.

"So, if you truly loved the one who has departed temporarily from you, send them loving thoughts; remember the good and wonderful things about them, and put aside all the things they did that were not so perfect.

"No human is perfect, Joanie, nor are we here. We are all learning to be better. That is what life is all about whatever plane it is on.

"The first thing, then," Scior continued, "that the ones left behind can do, is to send loving thoughts to the one who has just come over here. There's a period of adjustment on coming here, and the loving thoughts from those on earth help us here, for we, too, regret leaving those we love. Not only do we miss them, but the main reason for our regret is the unhappiness our departure has caused them."

"But how can we help but grieve, when we love someone?" I asked.

"We expect you to grieve," Scior answered, "that is natural, as

I said, but between the bouts of missing us, please send us some loving thoughts. They are of such tremendous help.

"Words are not needed. Just a warm feeling of love, coupled with the name or a visualization of the one here. This is more help than anyone on earth can imagine.

"Those left behind should remember that we want them to be happy—or as happy as they can be without us—and get on with their lives. We want to be proud of them and what they achieve on their own. And very often, when an entity comes here, if they wish it, they are trained and assigned guide status to the one they left behind, as I am to you.

"So, those on earth should remember that. They are probably more in touch and closer to their loved ones at this stage than they were when both of them were on earth."

Scior and I talked every evening. I sat at the typewriter, relaxed, lit my white candle, and asked if he were there. He always was. And the more we conversed, the easier it became.

A few weeks later I met Sylvia again for breakfast. Without preamble she suddenly said, "It's not Peter you're talking to, you know. It's what psychiatrists call active imagination."

"I'm not imagining it," I objected.

"No, I'm not saying you are," she replied. "It's coming from the collective unconscious. That's what Jung called it."

I decided not to argue. After all, I couldn't *prove* it was Peter. I felt I didn't have to. I *knew*. Just as a mother animal will recognize her own offspring in the seal breeding grounds among the thousands and thousands of pups, so I just knew it was Peter.

Maybe the information Scior was giving me was from the collective unconscious, but he was the channel for it, if you want to put it that way. And it was he who was contacting me, wherever the information came from. There was a closeness and a familiarity and a love that warmed me through and through.

I do not consider myself to be a particularly gullible individual. When, years before, in North Africa, receiving messages with the cup and the letters, and when I had been using the Ouija board by myself, both times the same message had been, "This is a clumsy way of communicating. Be still and I will come into your mind." But I had been too skeptical to even countenance doing that. I know how easy it is to deceive oneself, and find only what one wants to find.

A few months after Peter died, I had a young fellow painting the house, which definitely needed it. He was a good painter, but he was also a terrific con man. He was always needing money for this and that, for paint, to get the car repaired—and he was always going to pay me back from the next job. He stepped right into that huge, empty hole that Peter had left, and he needed nurturing.

The pièce de resistance was when he came around one morning early, sobbing his heart out. His mother had died and he needed money to fly back for the funeral. He sobbed on my doorstep for three days until I finally gave way and lent him some more. When he didn't return to town in the specified time, I phoned his brother, whose number he had left with me, and found out that their mother was as hale and hearty as I.

The painter left town soon after that and spent some time in jail in California from where he wrote to me, but I never replied. He left me the poorer by over $2,000, and I have never been conned by another human being since. As someone said to me, "An education costs, whether you get it in college or elsewhere."

So, I am especially aware of deceiving myself. I questioned over and over the fact that this was really happening to me. I was critical. I raised objections. And every time the answers came back, "No, this is not your imagination. You are not putting these words into your mind. It is I, Scior, talking to you."

It took many, many months before I felt really secure that this information was not coming from within myself, and all the reassurances would crumble now and again before my doubt.

Sometimes I would sit at the typewriter, typing away, and suddenly my mind would go blank in the middle of a sentence, and I would sit, silently, waiting for the next word to appear on the screen of my mind and be translated through my fingertips to the page. I had no idea what that word would be, but after a few seconds, out it came.

And through it all I felt Scior's love and care and concern.

A long time later, Sylvia happened to mention the subject again. I told her how much she had hurt me, how I felt as though she had slammed a door in my face, when all I wanted to do was to share something that I thought was wonderful.

"Well, I had to think about it," she said. "I have to think about things like that before I answer."

I hadn't realized. "Why didn't you say so, then?" I asked.

"Oh, I don't know," she answered. "I didn't think it was important."

It had been important to me, but, like Scior said, I have to be ·patient. Not everybody thinks alike, and what a dull world it would be if they did. I thought of all the good things I like about Sylvia, and what a terrific friend she is, how we laugh together, and if we don't see eye to eye on some things, well, we can just agree to differ. There's always room for another point of view. So, I continued with my nightly sessions.

By my typewriter I have pictures of Peter, taken at various times during our life together. They spread over the years; in one he is up his sister's tree gathering pecans, in another he is changing a flat tire on the car one time we were out. In others he is immersed in making a model on the back patio of our home, or conducting an experiment with paper and a pinhole in order to watch a solar eclipse. In one he is standing on the front porch with our cat, Bobbie, in his arms.

I remember the times I would be sitting at the typewriter, working, and things were not going well, and I would explode in frustration. He would enter the room quietly, come up behind me, put his hands on my shoulders, and say gently, "I'm sorry you're having a bad day."

In the years after Peter had gone, I would remember these things, and when I was sometimes in despair, I would also recall the words he had said to me so often, "Whatever else happens to you in your life, know that you have been LOVED."

As he had helped me, now I could help him by sending him loving thoughts.

Some people may think I should have let Peter go, to live his own life Over There, and I get on with mine. But I had let him go for ten years. Then he returned of his own accord.

# CHAPTER 5

## GETTING TO KNOW
## YOUR GUIDE

I often wonder, if I had not been so backward-looking, if I had not so immersed myself in despair and misery after Peter died, whether I would have regained my balance sooner. If I had known that he was there, waiting for me to make contact, I know I would have.

The tears dried up after several months—until then I cried nearly every day—but the loneliness, the empty ache never really went away. Oh, I would be around people and display a bright outside, and for a time the ache would disappear as I filled my thoughts with what was happening at that moment.

But when I returned home to the empty house, I could still see him coming down the hallway in his light-colored pants and khaki shirt that he loved to wear. I could still hear him puttering in his workshop, still see him on the patio working on making something for one of his models. It was then that the silence became deafening, and I would curl up into a little ball on the couch or the bed and reach out my hand to the empty air. The tears would well up in my eyes, and before I could stop them I was sobbing again.

They say the longest road has to turn sometime. My long road of unhappiness and loneliness ended after eleven years when I found I could contact Peter, or Scior, his new name.

When I was first able to contact Peter all the tears faded away.

My house felt a home again. It was as if he was still there, just out of my sight, as he had been when he was away working.

One evening I was talking to Scior and reminded him of all the times, as Peter, he had said to me, "Whatever else happens to you in your life, know that you have been LOVED."

"The minister quoted that at your funeral," I said. "Were you there? Had you recovered enough to be there?"

"Oh, yes," Scior replied, "I was there and I was very touched that you had told him that, and that he remembered.

"And thank you, too, for all the loving thoughts you have been sending me in the last few days. They are making such a difference."

"Do you still love me?" I asked.

"Of course I still love you. Don't I say so every time we talk?"

"Yes, you do, but sometimes you seem so far away. I guess I'm just feeling a little down tonight because I am tense."

"Joanie, you are my love and always will be. We have feelings here just as intense as those who are still in the body on earth. I know you miss the physical contact, the reaching out and touching, and I do, too, in a way. But I can feel, perhaps, closer to you now than you can feel to me, and it hurts me to think that you doubt that I love you."

"I don't doubt it, Scior. I suppose I just want to hear it more often because I am denied the touching of you and the seeing of you. I hear you, in my mind, but you had such a beautiful voice in your last body. I have a few minutes of it on a tape somewhere, and I play it sometimes, just to listen to that wonderful basso profundo."

"I love you. I love you. I love you. More?"

I felt better. "I believe you. I believe you. There, you are making me laugh, and that feels better."

"I'm glad," Scior replied. "I wanted to do that. Laughter is always good when it is wholesome and not disparaging."

"It is good to know that your love is still there and surrounding me."

"Of course it is, and it always will be."

"And don't forget that I love you," I told him. "That's very important."

"Indeed it is. It is this that helps me so much, your love, and your loving thoughts, and the contact we have. It makes it so much more wonderful now that we are in contact and you know I am there. That is what was important; that you know and recognize that I am here with you all the time."

"Had you been looking after me for a long time before we started these conversations?" I asked.

"Oh, yes, from almost immediately after I came here. Remember the scents? That was me, only then you were not so busy-minded and always busy, as you were later, for years, and it was easier to reach you, even though you did not have the strength to work the cup and the letters. But I have been with you almost from the day I came here."

I thought of the arid desert of time that had passed between then and now. "And it has taken over ten years for me to recognize that."

"Yes, sweetie, it has. But never mind, we are in contact now."

Another night, I was talking to Scior, when he said, "Tonight we will talk about angels."

"You mean like angels in heaven, flying about with wings and a white nightie?"

"Well," Scior hesitated, "that is what they are depicted as by some humans on earth, but they don't really look like that, as I'm sure you realize.

"But there are angels over here and they had to be presented in some way so that the people looking at the pictures would recognize something about them, and the presentation had to give some idea of how they operate. So, the artist had to use items that would be understood by those looking at the pictures, hence the wings.

"Perhaps if somebody were drawing an angel for the first time these days, they would have some sort of a back-pack that would enable them to fly. But the flying part is just to allow the viewer to realize that angels do not have to rely on the same ways of travel that humans do."

"Would you be called an angel?" I asked.

"Yes. An angel is really an entity over here that is doing helpful work for the earth, for humankind, the animals, the growing things of the earth, the ecology, and so on."

"Does a person ever have more than one guide at a time?"

"Sometimes. Occasionally there is a need for more than one guide because that particular person is going through a series of traumatic experiences and needs additional strength. In these cases more than one guide is allotted to them so that they can receive various kinds of strength to enable them to cope with the various stresses in their life."

"How does one receive a guide?" I queried. "Are all guides 'allotted,' as you just said, or can a guide choose the human they look after? How is this arranged?"

"Generally speaking, by compromise," Scior answered. "If there is a strong tie between an entity over here and a human, (as between you and me) then the entity here applies to take over the guidance of that human. If there is no objection from higher up, then that is set in motion.

"But in cases where a human does not have any ties to anybody in this dimension, then the entity here is asked to review the person on earth and see if they think they will be compatible to work with as a guide, and if the entity agrees, then that is settled."

"Are there any other reasons for a guide/human relationship?"

"Sometimes a guide is chosen for a human on the basis of what that human has to learn during the present lifetime, or what the human's interests are, where they may be led to a deeper interest in some subject, country, or occupation that has already caught their imagination or interest."

"How often does a human have a change in guides?" I asked.

"It varies," Scior said. "Sometimes a guide will stay with a human for most of their life. Sometimes a guide or a human finds the interaction is not compatible, in which case there is a parting of the ways, and another guide is assigned or chooses to take over that human."

"Is a guide usually the opposite sex of the human, or the same?"

"Well, we really don't have sexes here, but since an entity incarnating as a man will retain the outlook of a man when over here, and likewise with a woman, you could say that, in a way. The last incarnation," Scior went on, "leaves a mental impression with the entity over here and that tends to bring a more masculine or feminine outlook."

"And the outlook of the guide influences the human they are looking after?"

"A guide retaining the outlook of the opposite sex to the human they are guiding, creates a more balancing effect as that human progresses through life, simply because they are not thinking along the same lines, and can present a different point of view."

"Are there ever inefficient guides?" I wondered. "And if so, what happens when that occurs?"

"Occasionally, there are guides who do not function well in that capacity," Scior replied, "and then they are taken out of the circuit, as it were, and given further training, and tried again with another human.

"But you must remember not all humans are good at the same type of things, and it is the same here. We are not competent in every facet simply because we do not inhabit a body. There are some entities here who are suited to some type of work and not another. Because we no longer have a body, as you know it, does not make us superbeings."

"Oh! I kind of imagined you were."

"What? Superbeings? Oh, no, not at all, Joanie. We are learning here, just as humans are learning on earth. When you get into the hierarchy, then they are what you would call superbeings. But you were asking about guides, and some of us are suited to be guides, and some of us do other work."

"Does every human have a guide?"

"Oh, yes, always. There is never a human left to flounder alone through life.

"The hardest part of a guide's job is getting their human to tune in to them. Humans are always so busy, and rushing around. And if they are not rushing, then they are listening to music, or the TV, or chattering with friends.

"That is why it is so important to find some quiet time in your life if you wish to contact your guide."

"Is it always best to start with meditation?" I asked.

"Well, Joanie, there must be space in your thoughts for your guide to get through to you. Meditation, even for a short time every day, is a great help in other areas of life, too. Your health will improve, stressful situations will be less painful, you will sleep better, irritations will no longer plague you. In fact, there will be many benefits.

"Your guide cannot contact you unless there is space in your thoughts for an entry."

"But what should one actually *do* to start contacting your guide?"

"Sit quietly," replied Scior, "relax and tell your guide that you would welcome a contact. Do not expect lights to flash and bells to ring, not the first time, nor any time.

"But, if you remain quiet at a regular time over several days, your guide will make his or her presence known to you. It is a great help, when starting contact, if you light a white candle. This helps us to come through, for we can use the energy present in the flame.

"Your guide may advise you they are ready to talk to you by manipulating the candle flame, making it flicker (make sure there is not a draft), or suddenly flare up or die down. Or you may simply experience a sudden feeling of companionship or a closeness within you."

"And then" I interrupted, "what should a person do then?"

"When you believe your guide to be there, ask, 'Is my guide there?' and if you feel the answer to be 'Yes,' then greet them as you would a visitor to your home.

"We like to be welcomed," Scior continued, "for we do not wish to push in where we are not wanted or appreciated.

"The worst thing anybody can do is to make this into a parlor game and treat it as a lot of fun. If a human does that, it will be many, many years before the effect wears off and their guide will believe them to be serious about making contact.

"We are not playthings; the Cosmic is not a playground, though many people try to make it so. It is not likely that humans would mock prayer in a place of worship, and the principle of contacting your guide is the same. This is a serious matter.

"When a human has reached contact with their guide," Scior went on, "the next thing to do is to set up a regular time for contact, if that is what they wish to do. It can be as little as once a month, or once a week, or daily. Whatever is convenient. Although, like anything else, contact improves with practice, as you have found out, Joanie."

"Yes, indeed, I have," I answered. "It is so easy now to talk to you that I sometimes forget that you aren't around physically anymore."

"You do not have to have esoteric conversations with your guide," Scior continued. "It is our job to help you through life, and you can talk about any mundane matter that springs to mind.

"We are not a crutch, however, nor are we allowed to think for you; you have to make your own decisions. We can make suggestions, but we cannot force you to follow them. Your life is yours to lead however you think fit. We can advise you, but you do not have to follow our advice. It is up to you to make your own lifestyle."

"And when we have finished talking, what then?"

"When you have finished your conversation with your guide, thank your guide for coming to talk to you and for their input, and bid them goodbye, just as you would any other visitor to your home."

"There are some books," I put in, "that claim to tell you how to contact your guide and say that your guide is your slave."

"That is completely out of line," Scior said. "Not only are we not playthings, we are not slaves, either, and we will not take abu-sive language or orders.

"Any human who so treats their guide will not only sever the contact with that guide, but will attract other beings from a lower vibrationary level, which could cause problems of a grave nature."

"Suppose some people want to know their guide's name. It is much nicer to be able to talk to someone who has a name."

"Then ask the guide," replied Scior. "If the questioner is sin-cere, the name will be given. It may not be given the first time of asking, for a rapport has to be built up. A name is a very powerful thing, and not to be bandied about.

"Once you know your guide's name, it should not be broad-cast to all and sundry and boasted about, but kept close, and if told, only to those who you know will not abuse the trust."

# CHAPTER 6

## LISTENING FOR A BETTER LIFE

Now that I could talk to Scior I felt much more relaxed. The hassles and hummocks of everyday living were somehow smoothed out. I felt, no, I *knew* I was not alone; if I needed help and advice it would be there for the asking. I would sit in the living room in the evening, look up at the heavy beams in the ceiling, and think, "This is *our* home."

Oh, I knew the decisions and the work were up to me, but there was an indefinable moral support that I felt all the time. I would smile sometimes, to myself, just sitting there, because I felt loved, and protected, and cared for once again.

Sometimes, when I have a task to do I am not fond of, such as cutting the lawns (you try cutting the lawn when the temperature is 107°F!) I say, before I start, "Thank you, Scior, for helping me cut the lawns," and everything goes smoothly. The mower starts on the first pull, the string trimmer doesn't jam or run out of line half way through the job, the wind doesn't blow away my sweepings, just as I have them in a neat pile to dump in the trash bag.

One time when I was talking to Scior about the work guides do, I asked, "Is training given before an entity starts acting as guide to a human?"

"Oh, yes," Scior replied. "Being a guide is not something that comes naturally, like breathing to a human. We are always trained in everything we do, to try and make sure that we do the best job possible."

"Do some humans resist being guided?"

"Very definitely. It is distressing to some guides how they are unable to get through to their human protegé."

"What should we do to enable contact with our guide to be at its best?"

"The best way is to take a regular, short period of relaxation," Scior answered. "Relax the mind as well as the body. It is not necessary to sit in meditation, if that is not compatible with one's circumstances. But it is most necessary to still the mind for a certain period of time, and it is best if this can be done at a regular time each day, if possible.

"Busy-minded people," he went on, "always on the go, always thinking actively about things, are extremely difficult to contact, and it becomes very frustrating to a guide at times when they try to do their best, and can't get a word in edgeways, as it were. Five or ten minutes stilling of the mind each day would be of enormous benefit to both the guide and the human."

I remembered something I had read some time ago. "I have read reports," I said, "of business people who are very successful and they say, if they have a problem, they go into their office, shut the door, relax and—they don't say 'meditate'—but think about the problem, and the answer comes to them. They call it intuition. Would that be contact with their guide?"

"Oh, yes, definitely. That is part of our work. We plant suggestions, suggest opportunities or ways of overcoming a certain problem. But humans have free will. They can listen and take heed or not, as they choose. The successful businessmen or women are those who take heed, those who listen to the suggestions and act on them"

"But," I objected, "you said you were not allowed to help, and we had to make it on our own. Now, with the business people I mentioned, you help them. That seems a contradiction."

"Not really," Scior replied. "We are not allowed to provide material things (you mentioned winning a bunch of money to make life easier), because the things you achieve without any effort on your part are meaningless and teach you nothing.

"But we most certainly can help you if you will but listen. We plant suggestions in your mind; we provide mental support that makes you feel good and helps with unpleasant or irksome tasks. We can smooth your life this way. Do you not say every morning when you awake, 'Thank you, Scior, for smoothing my day,' and when you remember to do this, is not the day smoother?"

"Yes, indeed, it is."

"Help is always available, Joanie, but *you have to ask for it*. We cannot barge into your life and rearrange it for you. That would be interfering, and we are not allowed to interfere.

"We cannot influence you on earth as to what you should or should not do. You, yourselves, have to make the choices because you have the free will to do that, but if you open your inner ear and genuinely listen, then things will be made plain, and you will feel good about certain projects and bad about others, and the good ones are the ones to follow.

"If you ask for help," Scior went on, "it will always be given, but not in material form. The opportunities will be put before you, but you have to make the decisions and do the work to take advantage of those opportunities.

"But, even under these circumstances, you are still making the choice. It is just that you are listening more to the voices that would help you. And you can choose whether to listen or not."

"Thank you for helping me, Scior, every time I ask."

"Help is always there, Joanie, if you ask. Or if anyone asks their guide for help. It is always given. Only do not attempt to tell the guide how you would want this problem solved. There may be things that you do not know about in connection with this problem, things pertaining to other entities on earth, or another entity's karma, that your request may be affecting.

"Therefore, when you ask your guide for help, just ask for the desired result, and do not attempt to dictate how it shall come about."

"What other types of work do you do?" I wanted to know.

"As a guide?" Scior asked.

"Yes."

"We watch over our human and try to keep them from harm. If a child is in danger of, say, falling into the swimming pool, we try and get through to the mother and alert her to go and look for the little one.

"There is a very strong bond between a loving mother and her child, and that helps us to reach the mother.

"Sometimes it is a teenager we are looking after and he gets an urge to put his foot down in the family auto. For example, we can see that just around the curve in the road, one car is stupidly trying to overtake another, and if the teenager speeds up, there will be an accident. We try to get through to him and induce him to slow down. Sometimes he listens."

"Through all that loud rock music?" I muttered.

"There are always difficulties."

"What other things do you do?"

"We try and urge a young person to work hard in school or college and attain his or her dream. This requires constant application, for there are so many distractions for young people. But the ones who achieve their goals are the ones who listened to our suggestions."

I thought about the pain and emptiness of my life before I could talk to Scior. "What about the people who have been left behind?" I asked. "How do you try to help them?"

"As you know, Joanie, it is difficult very often to get through to those left behind because they are so sad. As I said, this is natural, and nobody can blame them. But if they would only give us some quiet time, it would help us to make an impression on their subconscious and get through to them and help them."

"Sometimes, Scior," I reminded him, "being quiet is one of the hardest things to do after we have lost someone we love. We keep thinking back and remembering, and keeping ourselves busy with something else helps to keep our mind away from who and what is now missing from our life."

"I understand, Joanie. And we appreciate that, believe me.

But if it would help to think of your loved one, happy and not suffering and eager to reach you, do you not imagine that would be an inducement to have a few quiet minutes every day in order to allow that contact to be made?"

"Yes," I answered, "I think it would. It would have been to me, had I known. When I did make contact with you and sat at the typewriter, the time just flew by and I never realized how fast it was going because I was happy, talking to you."

I had a sudden thought. "But suppose someone doesn't type. What then?"

"Typing is not necessary," Scior said. "You only do it to keep a .record of what we say. The conversations do not have to be recorded, they can be just conversations, as with anybody."

"But it was such a help to read over those things and go over what you had said. It made me feel so much closer to you."

"Then," Scior suggested, "if someone does not type or have a computer, use a tape recorder. A small, hand-held one would be ideal, so that when there is a pause, you simply put it on 'hold' and start recording again when you are speaking. They would have to start each question with the word, 'Question,' and each answer with the word, 'Answer,' or something like that, to keep things less complicated when listening to it. But that should not be a problem, especially after a little practice. Yes, I think that would be a good idea."

It is a good idea to keep a record, even if not a written one. I used to read through those sessions over and over, night after night, and I glowed inside, knowing that I was talking to my beloved.

I would sit, sometimes, leafing through my books that held the records of our conversations, and I felt I simply could not believe it. That was one reason I never told anyone, except Bill and Mary, and Sylvia. Who would believe me?

I wondered about this one time, so I asked Scior. "Just one thing I wanted to know. Are you cross with me for doubting that I am receiving these messages correctly?"

"Cross? No, sweetie, of course not. It is only natural that you should have some doubts at first; you are intelligent and this is, after all, somewhat new to you. It is not as if it has been happening all your life."

"What made this happen when it did?" I asked.

"Your pattern of living and your ways of thinking," he answered. "I had been trying for years to get through to you when you had recovered your strength after I died, but you were always so busy and wrapped up in your work that I could not break through. Otherwise this would all have been happening some time ago."

My questions ranged far and wide and covered many subjects. "Is there such a thing as the Recording Angel?" I wanted to know.

Scior was patient with me. "Every time you help somebody, that is a good deed on your record. The allegory of the recording angel, though not as factual as often depicted, does occur in principle."

"I know we are here on earth to learn," I said, "but how can we learn more and better?"

"Be aware that everything that seems bad to you when it happens—such as losing someone you love—is often meant as a learning experience. This may seem hard to some people, and indeed, it is a most difficult experience to work through, but everything happens with a purpose, and if you do not struggle, you do not learn very much, and it is by struggling and overcoming obstacles that you gain strength and grow.

"Remember," Scior went on, "that the child who does not exercise its muscles remains a weakling, and mental and spiritual muscles need exercising, too.

"Sometimes, losing a loved one can turn those who are left into an entirely different direction in life. They may work to eradicate drunken drivers from the road, for example, so that others will not suffer as they have done. They may be inspired to work for safer automobiles, or to erase the evil of drug dealers from their neighborhoods.

"Their pain and anguish has given them strengths they did

not know they possessed, and although they have lost something extremely precious to them, they are growing within by using that pain to gain the strengths necessary to do what they have to do."

"But sometimes," I said, "when we want very badly to do something, it seems as though all sorts of obstacles are put in the way, and we could take that as a sign that we are not supposed to do this particular thing."

"If you are not sure what it is that you are meant to do," Scior replied, "then open your inner ear, listen to the suggestions that come, and all will be made plain.

"You were unhappy at home, and yet did not really want to leave your comfortable and familiar surroundings, all your toys and treasures. But when you went to Bahrain, there were no regrets, no hesitating; it all seemed to fall into place. That is the kind of feeling you have to open up to."

"So, if a thing feels comfortable to us, then we should go along with it?"

"Precisely. If it doesn't feel comfortable, then discard it because it will never come out well for you."

# CHAPTER 7

## OVER THERE

When I was sitting by his bedside, watching my husband die, I had wondered what was going through his mind. I had wondered whether he knew I was there, whether he could hear me telling him that I loved him, whether he knew he was dying. Or was it just a blank? One evening I decided to ask him.

"Scior," I said, "what is it like to die? Do you feel anything? What happens?"

"My, what a lot of questions! Let's deal with them one at a time, shall we?" Scior answered.

"I did know you were there. I could hear you telling me you loved me, as you know by my bringing back my little magnets. I answered that question for you.

"What happens? Well, as the human senses fade, you begin to feel very light, light in weight, I mean, almost as if you were in water and floating to the top, very gently and calmly. I floated upwards, and when I did so, I could see you out in the hall and the doctors around the bed. But even before they pushed you out into the hall I was rising and leaving the body and only fraily connected. I could hear you telling me you loved me and that was a big comfort because I didn't really want to leave you. That's one reason I am so glad to have made contact with you again now."

"Did it hurt?" I wanted to know.

"Oh, no," Scior said. "There is no pain and no apprehension. There was somebody there with me, a sort of guide, and I was pulled along what seemed to be a long tunnel, that's the best way

I can describe it, pulled as if in a current. There was a bright light at the far end of the tunnel, and all the time there was this other person with me, explaining what was happening.

"Then other people joined us, explaining things and pointing out things, and comforting me, because there are regrets over here, too, about leaving loved ones, although we know it has to come about sometime."

I felt happy to know that this leaving of the body was something that was not terrible, and that Peter had been comforted because he was leaving me. I know how desolate I had felt in that hospital room right afterwards. It seemed as if the whole world had collapsed, and there was nothing firm and solid anymore. It was as though an invisible door had slammed down and cut me off from the one person in my life who truly meant something to me. If only I had known what was happening I would have looked around for him, and silently told him again that I loved him. But I could tell him now.

"I love you, Scior," I said interrupting his account.

"I know you do, Joanie, and I love you. You don't know how much it means to me to hear you say or think those words."

"Another point of light?" I queried.

"Yes, indeed, another point of light. The many times you tell me that, I am becoming like a star in the heavens."

"I'm sorry," I apologized. "I interrupted you. Please go on."

"Well," Scior continued, "there was a warm, loving feeling surrounding me, and somehow I felt at home, even though I was unhappy at leaving you. I was assured you would be looked after and was told that, in time, I may take a hand in looking after you, myself.

"Entities here—I can't really call them 'people' because people have bodies—were with me all the time, pointing out the beauties of the place, and explaining how to handle thought processes because, of course, there is nothing material here and everything is done mentally, as it were.

"Then, after a while, instruction began on the work I was to do."

"Looking after me?"

"Well, that is part of it."

"Early on in this contact, when Bill was there, at the start, you said that you were looking after soldiers from the Vietnam war."

"That is true, Joanie."

"How can you do both?"

I could almost feel Scior smile. "Time, as you know it," he explained, "does not exist here. Everything happens what you would call instantaneously. So do not worry that I will be neglecting you when I am helping soldiers from the Vietnam war."

"How do you help them?"

"Many of them are still bitter about the way they and their comrades were treated by the people back home. We have to try and get them over that, and heal the wounds in their thinking. You might almost call it psychological counseling."

"And it didn't hurt when you left the body?" I wanted to be sure.

"No, Joanie. It feels very good to be rid of pain when you come here. I mean pain in the body. It is like the relief you feel when you collapse in a chair after being tired and exhausted, only much more pronounced. It is a wonderful feeling to be here."

"You talked about the beauty of the place where you are. Can you tell me more what it looks like? Are there plants and trees?"

"Oh, yes," Scior responded, "and streams and mountains and rivers and oceans."

"Is it the same world that we see, only you see it differently?"

"Some of it is, but there are things we can see and you can't."

"Such as?"

"We can see the sap coursing through the veins in a leaf; we can see the heartbeat of a bird; we can feel the terror of a tree when the man with the chainsaw comes up to it."

"You mean that trees have feelings, like fear?"

"Oh, yes, Joanie. Plants and trees have feelings and emotions, just as you and I do. But we can sense them and feel them, and share their sorrow or joy. Very few humans can do this."

I remembered Cleve Backster and his experiments with lie detector equipment on plants, how they reacted to hurt, recognized people who had done them harm, and even reacted to the thought of hurting them.

And many years before him, Sir Jagadis Chandra Bose, the Indian physicist and plant physiologist, who invented extremely delicate and precise equipment to measure plant movement. He had been trained as a surgeon, but was so tender-hearted that he could not bear to cut into the living flesh, even to heal, so had turned to his second love, physics. He found that plants and trees had emotions, days when they felt blue and depressed, days when they were happy, and sad when a companion was removed.

"Are there animals there, where you are?"

"Yes, there are animals, all sorts of animals, but they lead a kind of separate existence; they come to learn, too, but in a different way. I can't explain."

My mind boggled. "I sometimes feel I am making this up."

"No, Joanie, you are not. Sometimes you are more relaxed than others and then it is easier to get through. Tonight you are not very relaxed."

I decided to take up this conversation another time when I *was* more relaxed. So, a few evenings later I brought up the subject again.

"You were talking the other night about how everything is mental where you are," I reminded Scior.

"Yes?"

"And then you were talking about the beauty of where you are, and that some of that is not what we see on earth. If everything is mental, how can you have mental mountains and streams and rivers, and things?"

"Thoughts are very powerful," Scior explained, "and if you hold a thought long enough and with sufficient concentration, it becomes permanent. There are no material mountains and streams and oceans here, but there has been so much concentrated thought spent on these things that they are now permanently visible to us. This has been going on for a very long time, remember," he added.

"Can anybody still in a body see them, ever?"

"Very occasionally," Scior replied, "in dreams. If you dream that you are with someone who has left the body and you are both in a very beautiful place, in all probability you are seeing something of what is here."

I went off on another tack. "Do you ever go and visit places on the earth that you would like to see, just for pleasure, or are all your journeys to do with work?"

"We can visit different places, if we want to," Scior said, "if we have an interest in them. We are not restricted in that way at all."

"Are you allowed time out, as it were, free time, when you are not looking after your protegé or working at your job, when you can do just what you would *like* to do?"

"Oh, yes," Scior responded. "We get free time, if you like to call it that. But we do not get tired, as humans do, so there is not the need to relax so much."

"But there is such a thing as mental tiredness."

"I agree, and that is why we are allowed time off, as you put it, and someone else fills in for us for a while. But things happen so fast over here, not like earth time, that only a very short while in your time is needed for us to refresh ourselves."

"Do entities there, guides and others helping people, ever get burned out? Or what we on earth call burned out?"

"Sometimes," Scior replied, "and then they are taken off the job, as it were, and given a real rest. If an entity or a human is burned out, they cannot do a really good job, and it is important that we do a good job here."

I remembered the death of my mother and something I had read in the paper. "I was reading the other day about people who seem to stave off dying because of some personal thing they want to wait for, like seeing someone they love, or because of a particular holiday or observance. And this seems to happen in many cases. How do they do that?"

"Through their mind," Scior answered. "You know how powerful your mind is. Your mother put off dying until you arrived to see her, otherwise she would have been over here several days earlier."

"I always thought that she did; I just had that impression."

"The absolute date of passing over is not set in concrete, so to speak," Scior went on, "and a human can put off the passing for a small amount of time through the idea in the mind that they want to see someone, or go through a holiday or religious observance just one more time. We understand."

Another evening, I had other thoughts on my mind. "Do you see me all the time?" I wanted to know. "What I look like, what I am wearing, and all that sort of stuff?"

"Oh, yes, I can see you."

"Does that mean you can see other people, in fact, all people, too?"

"Yes."

"Do you ever feel that you are sort of snooping?"

"No, we are not snooping," Scior said. "This is our job, to watch over you, and when I say 'you' I mean it in the general sense."

"Do you have other people to watch over besides me?"

"No," Scior replied, "it is on a one-on-one basis."

"Contacting you has been such a help to me," I said one day to Scior. "Is it possible for anyone to do this?"

"Yes," he replied, "if they are truly wanting to make contact, and are persistent in their practice. As I have said many times before, it is our job to try to help you along the paths of life, and if you are in contact with us, how much easier it is for both of us. We are always there, if you will but listen to that small, inner voice."

# CHAPTER 8

## NO GRAVE, NO NOTHING

I have tried, ever since, to listen for that small, inner voice, as Scior called it, and whenever I ask for help, it is there. Whether it is smoothing the path of life or making me feel better inside—which is almost the same thing, really—it works. For, if you feel good inside, the other things of life progress much more smoothly.

Sometimes, the knowledge of his presence is so strong and tangible that I can almost feel the touch of his hand and hear that dearly beloved voice talking to me.

I do not have to sit down at the typewriter to talk to Scior; it happens anywhere and at any time. I can be driving along in the car, and make an inward remark to myself, perhaps about the beauty of the clouds over the mountains, and I feel the response, for Peter, too, loved beautiful things.

The first time I saw the great Colorado River, tamed and chained at the Hoover Dam between Nevada and Arizona, I cried. It was so smooth and deep and powerful on the one side, and on the other, so small and narrow. I gazed at the towering cliffs on the downside of the dam, and thought of the men who must have clung like flies to the canyon walls while erecting the steel stanchions that carry the electric cables.

I said to Peter, "America is so *big*. It makes me feel so small." He had put his arm around me and there were tears in his eyes as he said, "I love you, Joanie." He understood what I was feeling.

Peter had always been so understanding, so patient, so sensitive, and even though he was not physically with me any longer, those qualities still came through in our conversations. They gave a unity to my life that had been missing for so long; they soothed me when people aggravated me; they sustained me when I became lonely.

Peter had been in the Army, an Engineer in World War II, and he had seen a lot of action. The horror of it never left him, and he would talk by the hour sometimes of this incident or that, wrong decisions made by Command, buddies who couldn't be bothered to take cover, and died as a result.

Some of his stories were humorous, such as the time, during training in England, when everyone was going out on night maneuvers with a full pack. They would march twenty or more miles, but somehow he always managed to come back much jauntier than the others. One day somebody asked him how he did it.

"Well, I don't carry a full pack," said Peter.

"But you must. I've seen you with it."

Peter shook his head, laughing. All the equipment they were supposed to carry was finally wrapped in their shelter half (the half of a small tent that they were supposed to join up with someone else to use) so that none of it was visible and was protected from the rain.

Peter worked in the machine shop. "I don't carry a full pack," he said, laughing again. "I've made myself a frame out of welding wire, just the shape of a pack. When it's covered with my shelter half and pulled tight, nobody can spot the difference."

From then on he was kept busy making pack-shaped frames to be carried on night maneuvers. He could hardly keep up with the demand.

But a lot of his memories were not so happy, and one day, at the typewriter, I talked to him about this.

"You know," I said, "funerals are for the living, and visiting a grave helps the one who is left behind, but what about all those poor souls who lost somebody during a war? Very often they don't have any grave to go to, or even ashes. Sometimes the fighting man or woman or nurse was just 'missing.' There wasn't anything to

send back. What about these people? How can they help themselves endure the grief?"

There was a pause before Scior replied. "I know, Joanie," he
answered, "our thoughts go out to these poor people so very much.
I know you kept a lot of my things and were happy to have them
around—"

"I used to wear your shirts, sometimes, just to feel closer to
you," I put in.

"—but some people prefer not to do that. However, when
things are taken away, by force, as it were, it makes the one left
behind feel so deprived. Even if they had wanted to keep something," Scior went on, "they cannot. There was no saying goodbye,
very often no premonition, no approaching signs. The word came
like a gangland gunshot. And it was a terrible shock."

"But what can they do?" I persisted. "They have no grave, no
urn."

"But I am sure they must have a photograph of some sort,
perhaps more than one. If they wish, it is quite a good idea to
make a small collection of these photographs. Stick them on a
card, or put them in a large frame, and make a small shrine out of
them. They can put flowers or a plant by the photographs. Make
it look as attractive as possible in whatever way they want. They
can go to this quiet corner as if they were going to a grave.

"When they look at the photographs, they can send their missing loved one loving thoughts. It is the loving thoughts that are
the help, not necessarily the trip to the grave. And loving thoughts
can be sent very well, when looking at a photograph as well as at a
grave marker.

"In fact," Scior continued, "with a small shrine like that in a
home, looked at and loved very often, an aura of love is built up
around it, for thoughts are powerful things, and nothing that is
given is ever lost.

"So, think that with this build-up of loving thoughts, the same
will be returning to the sender from the one who is missing. Love

is never a one-way street, and whatever you give out returns to you over and over again."

I knew this to be true. Ever since sending loving thoughts to Peter, or Scior, as I now call him, I have felt his love around me every day.

My health improved. My outlook on life improved. My patience improved. And it all came from knowing that I was loved again. That someone was there, beside me, as he had been in times gone by, supportive, caring, and oh, so loving.

# CHAPTER 9

## A NEW BIRTHDAY

One evening I was feeling somber. I had been remembering a girl I used to be at school with when I was young. She was the daughter of our local hairdresser, and we parted company when I was age fourteen and my family moved to another part of the country.

Many years later we paid a return visit to the small town where I spent my early years, and were astounded to learn that Irene had committed suicide. She had married and apparently seemed very happy. She had an adorable two-year-old son and a husband who idolized her. One day her husband came home from work to find Irene hanging from the upstairs banisters. Nobody could understand why she had done it. I decided to ask Scior.

"You say there is a reason behind everything, Scior," I said, "but what about suicides? The suicide of someone you love is very hard to take."

"The suicide of someone you love," Scior answered, "is devastating to deal with because it seems a rejection of the love that others have given to the one who sought death. And nobody likes being rejected."

"What can they do," I asked, "those left behind? Can they still try to contact the one who has died or, because it was suicide, is there some restriction?"

"There is no restriction as far as contacts to be made," Scior replied. "We do not judge those who come over here; they judge themselves when they look back over their life just ended. Then it is up to the individual to decide what they want to do about it."

"Is suicide frowned on, as it were, in your dimension?"

"We do not judge those who come here, Joanie. It is a great pity when a human decides to leave their body of their own free will before it is their time. They are missing out on so much."

"But, sometimes people feel that the struggle is just too much for them, that life never seems to get better, and there is only one way out of their difficulties."

"There would have been other ways, Joanie, if only they had listened. But when they come here, that time is come and gone, and we have to think of their friends and relatives left behind."

"What is the best thing for their relatives to do?"

"The first and most important thing for them to do, is to send the one newly arrived here many, many loving thoughts. This is extremely important, for they left the body because, in part, they felt abandoned, or outside the mainstream of life, to put it another way.

"Maybe they had feelings of worthlessness; feelings of failure, either in their work or life, or living up to the expectations of others. They need the feeling of being loved almost more than any other entity here."

"There has been a lot written recently about teenage suicides," I said. "This must be something terrible for the parents to endure. And why? I know teenagers sometimes have a lot of pressure, but they have their whole life ahead of them."

"True, Joanie, but often teenagers will decide to leave the body because of reasons that, if they were more mature, would not push them into this decision. They have had little experience of life at their age, and problems and setbacks loom extremely large in their minds."

"But this is such a permanent solution to what is usually a temporary problem."

"Teenagers don't see it as a temporary problem, Joanie. To them it is the end of the world."

"And the parents? How can they help themselves over this?"

"First, by sending loving thoughts," Scior replied, "and then, when they have recovered a little, perhaps turning this tragedy into a learning experience."

"Sometimes, some parents are so wrapped up in their own affairs and coping with their problems, that they do not really notice what is going on with their teenage child. If they have other teenagers in the home, we hope that this dreadful experience will make them more aware.

"Sometimes, when it is an only child that dies this way, the parents turn their anguish into working to teach other parents how to look for signs that their child may be thinking of doing this.

"Many people never imagine that it will happen to one of their family members. These things happen only to other people, they think. That is never true, Joanie."

"And doing something positive like this would help to ease the heartache?"

"Yes, indeed," Scior answered. "Positive action is a great help in sorrow.

"In the beginning this may not be possible. Most parents are too devastated by this occurrence. But as time passes, helping others avoid what they have gone through is a tremendous aid in healing their shattered dreams."

"And when the suicide is not a child, but an older person, does the same principle apply?

"Oh, yes, Joanie. Helping others is always a great healer. Sometimes, with an older person, say, anyone from their thirties on up, if they are living alone for some reason, and have few friends, they feel abandoned. Sometimes their friends and relatives are so busy with their own lives that they forget to contact the one who is living alone, and then that person feels deserted."

"Everyone needs human contact. Loneliness is a terrible thing to endure," I said.

"Yes, Joanie. That is why, when something like this happens, the loving thoughts sent here are so very important."

In the years before Peter died we had both known his health

was deteriorating. He had gradually become weaker and weaker and able to do less and less. We had both known it was only a matter of time.

He spent many hours lying on the bed or on the couch in the living room, and one time, when I was leaving for the market he said, "Don't be too long, Joanie. I don't want it to happen while you're away." He must have been feeling particularly depressed that day because he never complained as a rule.

I remember one evening when I was washing up the supper dishes at the kitchen sink, he had come into the kitchen behind me. He put his arms around me and said, as he had so often done, "Did you know I was in love with you?" Then he collapsed on the kitchen floor.

I remembered those days now. "What about people who are terminally ill," I asked, "like those in hospices? Sometimes they linger for such a long time, and in terrible pain. Would it be a help for those who love them to talk about making contact after they have left the body?"

"I am sure it would, Joanie," Scior replied. "When someone is terminally ill, they know they are going to be leaving behind those they love and, as I said before, we, here, regret leaving those we love, just as you, still on earth, grieve over your loved ones not being around in the flesh anymore.

"If both parties would be willing to accept the idea that contact can be made after one has left the body, it would be of great help in making that contact afterwards. And it would probably happen much sooner than otherwise."

"We were talking about suicides earlier on," I reminded him. "What about those terminally ill folks who ask a doctor to help them out of this life? Most of these cases are considered crimes here. Do you think it a crime?"

"As I said, Joanie, we do not judge people here, but the doctor, remember, is only using his skills to alleviate suffering, which is what he is supposed to do. If the only way really to do that is to bring the invalid over here, then he is doing something good, in spite of earthly laws."

"But friends and relatives can still contact them, can't they?"

"Oh, yes, of course, Joanie."

Again I remembered how I had felt when Peter actually died. Even though I had known it was coming, part of me denied it, always hoping that he would get better and come home again.

"But even when we know that someone is going to leave us, when it actually happens, the feeling is terrible," I reminded him. "When you finally died, I felt as though the world had ended."

"I know, Joanie."

"I was glad you weren't suffering anymore, not in any more pain, but I still felt terrible. I suppose I was just feeling sorry for me."

A feeling of warmth and love engulfed me. "No, Joanie, you were not just feeling sorry for yourself. When two people love each other, there is a psychic bond between them that has nothing to do with man-made laws or regulations. And when that bond is broken by one leaving the body, it is natural that the other should feel very badly.

"You have heard of people who have a limb amputated but can still feel the pain in that limb, even though it is not physically there?"

"Yes, I have, Scior."

"The medical profession call that 'psychic pain,' and if this can be felt by the loss of a limb, how much greater must be the psychic pain when a psychic part of you, the whole you, departs.

"That is what happens when one of two or more loving people leaves the body, because those who love each other have a psychic entity that is a whole entity made up of the two halves, one half for each of them.

"No, Joanie, you were not indulging in self-pity. It was a real amputation, if you like to put it that way."

"And this is felt by anybody who loses someone they love?"

"Yes, Joanie, it is."

Many years ago, I remember reading a book called "Many Lifetimes" by Denys Kelsey, a psychiatrist and a member of the Royal College of Physicians in England, and his wife, Joan Grant, a gifted psychic. They wrote alternate chapters, detailing their lives.

Joan Grant recounted one incident that happened when she was a child. She had been psychic for as long as she could remember, and on this particular occasion had been allowed to attend a luncheon party her parents were giving. Among the guests was a prominent local doctor.

Suddenly Joan Grant realized that the doctor sitting opposite her at the table was going to die that night. Since nobody that she knew went to church, and she had never received any religious instruction, she thought that even the stupidest adult knew that between bodies they went to the Beautiful Country, which was her name for the place.

She thought it was a good idea, therefore, to congratulate the doctor on the fact that tomorrow would be his happiest birthday.

He told her that the next day was not his birthday, and she hurriedly explained that she meant the kind of birthday that happened on the day you died.

Her mother was outraged and she was immediately dismissed from the dining table, followed by her mother who berated her for making such a cruel remark and gave her a lecture on trying to draw attention to herself by saying such a thing. Later, when her mother had calmed down a little she rationalized that Joan had probably done no harm because the doctor was young and healthy.

However, all changed in the morning when news arrived that the doctor had been found peacefully dead in his bed.

So, now, instead of thinking that such-and-such a day is the day Peter died, I think of it as his new birthday, a birthday into another, more fulfilling life. No longer imprisoned in a pain-wracked body, no longer suffering disappointments and upsets, unemployment and the accompanying fears, he is free.

Therefore, try to think of the day your loved one departed the body as the day that something especially nice happened to them—

good for them. And if we *really* love someone, is it not good things that we wish for them, even though it costs us in the process?

To me, this is the essence of love, real love, the giving, even though sometimes it hurts.

We shall come through, for we know that our loved ones would want it. They would not want us to be mournful and dreary, mourning forever.

They need us to release them to continue whatever work they have to do as they follow the path of advancement.

# CHAPTER 10

## THE BUD UNBLOOMED

Several years ago Peter and I had gone to the coast for a long weekend to visit some friends. We had been home about two or three days when a letter arrived from my brother, Michael. Peter was at work when it came. Letters from my brother were rare, and I opened it with joy.

The letter was quite short. He told that their little girl, Tania, had been run over outside their house. He finished with the words, "If God exists, he must have needed a very special angel very quickly."

I was horrified. I phoned England immediately, and through my tears talked to Michael and his wife, Renate. They lived in the country, on a narrow, winding lane. Tania had been running home from the field opposite when her mother called her in for supper, and darted right in front of the car. The driver had no chance to avoid her. And what made it worse for him was that he had a little girl of his own, the same age as Tania.

"We have Tania upstairs," Michael told me. "She's wearing her favorite dress and her favorite hair ribbon. And we take turns sitting with her and reading to her."

I was devastated. Michael hadn't been home when this happened, he was working late. He arrived to find several police cars outside the house, and was greeted with the terrible news.

The accident had happened in front of her mother, and a neighbor immediately phoned for the ambulance and followed in his car with Renate. They waited outside the emergency room, going through heaven only knows what hell.

Finally the doctor appeared. Without softening the blow, he said brusquely, "Your daughter is dead."

The neighbor said later he could hardly restrain himself from punching the doctor. Emergency crews are always under pressure; maybe the doctor had been through a bad day. But surely, there was no need to be so callous.

When I had put the phone down, I could do little work. I kept thinking of my brother and his wife and young son. I knew Tania's bedroom, and in my mind I could see her lying on the bed in her favorite dress and hair ribbon, and either her mother or father sitting by the bed reading to a dead child. My heart broke, not only for this little life cut short so soon, but for her parents and brother.

When Peter arrived home and I told him, he, too, was very upset. He was quiet all evening, and when I mentioned that to him he said, "I keep thinking of Michael and Renate."

Somehow it seemed worse to me because we had been away at the time it happened, enjoying ourselves, never knowing what they were going through. Tania was seven years old.

The phrase in Michael's letter about a very special angel stuck in my mind for years, and one evening I raised the subject with Scior.

"You said that you were acting as my guardian angel," I began, "would all the entities over there, like you, be regarded as angels?"

"Yes," Scior answered, "we are all angels in that we are in this dimension."

"Would that apply even to children who leave the body?"

"Oh, yes, indeed."

"I've been thinking," I went on, "losing a child is a terrible thing for parents to undergo. What can anybody say or do to help them? It is something that must scar their lives forever."

There was a pause. Then Scior replied, "We all feel very deeply for these poor people. This is one of the hardest burdens to bear and one which, to the grieving parents, seems senseless, reasonless, and without cause.

"This early cutting-off of life, this snatching away of a bud before it has bloomed is one of the saddest times that can happen to a human."

"Why, Scior?" I asked. "Why does it happen?"

"There are many explanations," Scior responded, "but none of them makes any sense to the stricken parents or in any way alleviates their loss."

"Would it not help to know why they have to suffer this?" I queried. "Often, if someone knows the reason for something it helps them to accept it."

"True, Joanie, but this is a hurt that goes so deep, that rational or even spiritual explanations do not carry much weight. The only thing I can say is, that when they arrive here, then will they know the explanation."

"And in the meantime, all they can do is suffer?"

"No, Joanie, they can try to contact their child by the methods we have discussed."

"But how can they have a conversation with, for instance, a one-year-old?"

"Because there is no 'old' or 'young' here," Scior said. "Although the parents were not able to talk with their one-year-old when in a body, that one-year-old here is a mature entity. They should think of their baby or child as an angel, which, in truth, they are. If they follow the suggestions of relaxing and listening, they should be able to make contact.

"The first contact I would suggest they try to make is with their guide, who would then be able to aid them in contacting the entity who briefly inhabited the body of their lost baby or child or teenager."

"I think it must be difficult for a parent to think of their helpless child as a mature entity," I objected.

"I realize there may be difficulty," Scior replied, "but, believe me, it is the truth.

"The mature entity here chose the parents for some reason, chose to enter their baby's body as it was born. But the reasons, whether pertaining to the child or to the parents, are seldom disclosed to those still in the body."

"Sometimes, Scior," I said, "losing a child is such a devastating event to the parents that they end up divorcing. Is there something that parents can do to prevent this? Surely, both of them need support and love from the other at a time like this?"

"That is true, Joanie. And it is the hurt that bites so deeply that causes the breakup. People in these circumstances," Scior continued, "often blame the other spouse, either justly or unjustly. They feel so distraught that they lash out at the nearest and closest available being, trying in some way to alleviate the hurt they themselves feel.

"Perhaps they feel guilty themselves. Perhaps they feel they could have been more loving to the child, or less indulgent, or given the child more of their time. Or maybe they did something that inadvertently and innocently contributed to the death of that child, for which they unjustly blame themselves."

"What can someone in this position do to help with those feelings?"

"They should try to remember," Scior answered, "that all things happen with a purpose. They will not know that purpose, but they can try to be calm and listen for their inner voice, their guide, who is trying desperately to get through to them to offer help. Nothing can bring back their child, but listening for their guide's voice will help them deal with their loss and the anguish it has plunged them into."

"But Scior," I said, "very often parents put so much of their hopes and longings into a child, very often wanting to give the child better things, and opportunities, and a better life than they themselves had, and in this way fulfilling their own dreams. Now, all this is taken away."

"Not really, Joanie. Their hopes and longings can still be fulfilled, even though it is not through their own child, which would, of course, be the ideal situation.

"But these parents can adopt, they can act as a foster parent, they can approach an orphanage or a children's home and, even if they do not want to formally adopt a child, they can still bring it gifts, take it places, buy it clothes, help to give it a better education or special education, such as dancing or engineering, or something that the child shows a particular aptitude for.

"They can still give that child the love and care that they would have lavished on their own, and which a child in an institution, of necessity, lacks so much.

"Of course, there is always the possibility that they will have another child themselves."

"But it can never take the place of the one that was taken away from them, can it, surely?"

"No, Joanie, it cannot. Nor should the parents try to think that it could. This would be another child, another entity, probably with different tastes, talents, likes and dislikes, but still needing their love and care and affection."

I thought for a moment. "If these parents have no adult image of their child, how can they envisage a mature angel, which their child now is? How would they know it was their child?"

"It would be conveyed to them mentally," Scior said.

"I don't *see* you," I put in, "but I have memories of how you looked. People need something to visualize, some image that means something to them."

"Perhaps," Scior replied, "but these parents should not think of their lost one as a baby angel. As I said, we do not have age here. That is a requisite of earth. But there would be something about their contact that would make them realize this is their child.

"You do not see me, you said. How, then, do you think of me in this dimension?"

"That's tough to answer," I said. "I don't have a visual image of you over there. It's just a knowing, a feeling, like listening to you when you used to say, 'I love you.' I don't think of you now as some spirit, vaporous, whatever. I simply *feel* your presence."

"That, then, is what the parents would feel, Joanie. You know from your own experience that visualization of a particular person is not absolutely necessary. Sure, if it is an adult that leaves the earth plane, the relatives and friends have an image of them as they used to be, but they do not need to imagine that same body floating in the ether, as it were. You do not. You are simply aware of my presence in your mind.

"That is what the parents of a departed child would feel. Sometimes the loss of a child draws the parents closer together; sometimes it is the other way. But if only they both would listen for the comfort and help we are longing to offer, they would not break apart."

"Is there a time limit to this?" I asked.

"A time limit to what?"

"A time limit to making contact with their little one. Does this attempt have to be made soon, Scior, or can it be made months or years later?"

"It can be made anytime," Scior answered. "Immediately following a loss such as this, most parents are too debilitated, too distraught to be able to relax and concentrate. Sometimes it does take years to reach the state of calm and balance necessary to make contact. No, the length of time that has elapsed should not prevent them from making an attempt to communicate."

I knew what Scior meant. I did not have the strength following his death to make contact, and his departure was not the shock that losing a child must be.

Scior butted into my thoughts. "One more thing, Joanie, I said I could not tell all the reasons that this loss occurs, but one reason I can give you, and that is that there is some special child in the world who needs the love and care of these particular parents.

"Sometimes the entity here who inhabits briefly the body of the child who was lost to this couple, departs so that their love and tending can be given to this special child who needs it so much."

"But how would they know?" I wondered.

"If they listened to their inner voice, they would be led to that child who needs them," Scior explained. "The child the couple lost agreed to come to earth for a short while in order to act as the catalyst for the transfer of loving energies to the child who needs them so desperately."

"Could this not be achieved in a less devastating way?" I wanted to know.

"Sometimes that is not possible," Scior replied, "and remember, this is only in a few specific cases.

"People should try to treat everything that happens to them as a learning experience, and attempt to find out what they are supposed to do with the experience, although at the time it seems unbearable to them.

"The Cosmic is not capricious. There is a reason behind everything, even the terrible things that happen—or what humans regard as terrible.

"One day the pattern of their life will be made plain. Often unexpected strength comes out of adversity, if the recipient of the adversity will allow it."

# CHAPTER 11

## ANGEL CONTACTS

History tells us of many instances where guardian angels or angels have comforted and helped those on earth, just as Scior helps and comforts me.

The word angel is derived from the Greek *angelos*, which comes from the Hebrew *mal'akh*, usually translated as messenger. If 'messenger' relates to messages from that inner voice, then that meaning would be very applicable.

But originally angels were not thought of only as messengers; they did all sorts of work. And angels are not limited to Christian thought. There are references to angels in the Jewish and Muslim faiths, too, from earliest times. In fact, most religions through the ages have heavenly messengers incorporated into their teachings. Among other things, they were described as guardians, helpers, sustainers, and protectors.

Through the ages men and women have talked and written about their experiences with angels. Sometimes they see the angel, sometimes they simply feel a presence, as I felt one once.

Peter and I had been going through a bad period. Money was short, work was low, Peter was not well and needed an operation but kept refusing to see the doctor.

Actually, he had agreed the previous week to visit the doctor, but before we could make the trip, an old friend had dropped in, out of the blue, and stayed several days. By the time he had departed Peter had changed his mind again. Doctors were for when you had a broken leg—hernias didn't count!

That evening, he was lying in bed and I was overwhelmed with the enormity of our situation. I went out into the dark garden and put my arms around the trunk of a big, old elm. I laid my forehead against the rough bark and cried. The tears trickled down my face and onto my shirt. "Help me," I sobbed. "I don't know what to do anymore. Somebody, please help me!"

Immediately I felt a presence behind me. I knew someone was there, just as strongly as I knew Peter was lying in the bedroom. I didn't have to check to see if he was still there—I knew he was. It was with the same certainty I *knew* there was someone behind me.

A sense of calm and peace flooded over me. I knew my cry had been heard and heeded. I knew some solution would come. I knew everything would be all right.

The next day, a Friday, Peter didn't feel well. He stayed in bed. Saturday he felt worse, and by the time Sunday arrived he was sure he was dying. I suggested the emergency room, but he would have none of it. He hated hospitals.

Monday morning at 6:00 a.m. I phoned our doctor and, of course, got his answering service. They said he would call. I phoned my work place and told them I would be late, my husband was ill and I was waiting to talk to the doctor.

Time passed. Eight o'clock, nine, ten. At eleven o'clock I again called the doctor's office. When I spoke to the doctor and he found out that he had never received my message he was furious with his answering service. I told him of the situation.

"Let me talk to Peter," he suggested. I went into the kitchen and listened on the extension phone.

Peter wanted the doctor to make a house call. The doctor tried to persuade Peter to go to the hospital and meet him there.

"No, no," Peter said. "Why can't you come here?"

"Well," replied the doctor, "I can come and hold your hand and talk to you and charge you a bunch of money, but unless you come into the hospital I can't really tell what's the matter now. And if you come into the hospital," he added, "you know what I'm going to do—that little operation."

"Oh, no!" You would have thought Peter was being threatened with execution.

"Lots of people have a hernia repair," the doctor reasoned. "If you let it go much longer it could cause a much worse problem."

"Sometimes it goes away," Peter objected.

"And often it doesn't. Right?"

Peter mumbled something.

"Well," the doctor went on, "if you won't come into the hospital today, I can't tell you what's wrong at the moment. Would you prefer to lie there and suffer?"

"No," Peter moaned. "No."

"Well, come on, then." I thought the doctor was being very patient.

Finally, Peter agreed to go into the hospital that morning. The doctor said he would meet us there, which he did.

After Peter was settled in his room the doctor came to talk to me.

"What was the matter with him—apart from the hernia?" I asked.

"Absolutely nothing," replied the doctor. "I couldn't find anything wrong at all. I'll put it down as a virus infection," he added.

My plea for help had been answered, and in a way that I would never have envisaged.

Sophy Burnham, after writing "A Book of Angels," received so many letters from readers about angel contacts they themselves had experienced, that she brought out another book, "Angel Letters," made up entirely of extracts from these readers' letters.

Back at the typewriter, another point came to mind one evening.

"There is another question I want to ask, Scior," I started.

"Yes?"

"When we lose someone we very often feel a sense of guilt that we did not do this, that, or the other for the person while they were alive. How can this guilt feeling be alleviated?"

"By asking for help," Scior responded. "If you ask for help it will always be given—in some way, perhaps that you do not even imagine. And those left behind should always send the one here loving thoughts. That is a great dispeller of guilt because you are doing something positive for the one you love."

I thought a moment. "But if the one now over there is what we would call an angel, do they really need our loving thoughts?"

"Of course, they do. Yes, indeed."

"But you're *angels*." I felt puzzled.

"That doesn't mean to say that we don't appreciate your help. There are different types of angels," Scior explained, "just as there are different types of work on earth.

"If you go into a department store," he went on, seemingly changing the subject, "are you satisfied with the service you receive, as a general rule?"

"Oh, yes. I usually have no complaints unless it is something out of the ordinary."

"Right. You do not expect the executive in his suite of offices, controlling the destiny of the store, to come down and deal with your needs, do you?"

"No."

"And you would be very surprised if the president of the company left his office in Houston or wherever and flew specially to your town to sell you something?"

I laughed. "Indeed I would."

"Well," Scior continued, "if there is a hierarchy on earth in the way things are managed, do you find it so difficult to imagine the same idea is observed here?"

"No, I suppose not. That makes sense."

"There is great order in the universe," Scior said, "and this means that there are many types of angels. We, on this level, are like the salespeople in the store, serving the needs of our protegés.

"There is a chain of command here, just as in the store. Just as the salesperson is responsible to his or her supervisor or manager, so we, too, are responsible to those higher in the chain of command."

"So, even if you are an angel, there are angels over you?"

"Certainly," Scior replied. "And we need your loving thoughts, just as the salesperson appreciates a smile and a kind word."

"Oh! I hadn't realized that. I suppose I hadn't even thought about it."

"Angels," Scior explained, "are simply the entities who inhabit this level of vibration."

"Just as the people on earth are humans?"

"Right, Joanie. You might call it a generic term these days. Just as you, on earth, have the mineral kingdom, the plant kingdom, the animal kingdom, and the human kingdom, so are we the angel kingdom."

"With a structure of command?"

"Absolutely. There is always order. Otherwise there would be chaos."

When he explained it like that it all seemed so simple and matter-of-fact.

"Are the people who sense or see angels something special?"

"No, Joanie, not at all. They are simply people who have a need, just as you had a need that night out in the garden by the tree.

"If someone has a need and asks for help, you can depend on it that an angel will come to help them. It may not be immediate, just as yours was not immediate, but it will come. Sometimes, if the need is urgent, as when some danger is present, then the help will follow at once.

"But often, you know," Scior continued, "these things are arranged so that they do not appear as angel visitations to others. They will appear as ordinary happenings. Only the one who asked for help will realize the significance of what has happened."

"We were talking about guilt a little while back," I said. "Do you, over there, ever feel guilty, too?"

"Oh, yes, indeed, we do," Scior answered. "Often we reflect on the things we could have done for those we were living with or in contact with, or how we could have behaved differently while we were in the body."

"And do the loving thoughts help with that?"

"Yes, Joanie, they do. That is one reason they are so important. Just as those still on earth cannot now change their actions toward the one who has gone from them, we, too, cannot rectify our mistakes. But we do have the chance of helping those we love by acting as their guide or joining with others in aiding them in some way."

"Do you send us loving thoughts?" I asked.

I felt a warm glow around me as Scior replied, "Of course we do, Joanie. I send you loving thoughts every day, all the time. And when you look at one of the photos of me that you have around the house, I feel your loving thoughts and send mine back to you."

"As I sit at my typewriter I have several photos on the wall in front of me," I told him.

"I know," Scior replied. "And believe me, they are a huge help. They help you, not only when you look at them, but they help me, because when you look at them there is that warm, little feeling in your heart as you remember me."

"You said love is a two-way street," I reminded him. "And since I have been able to talk to you I can feel your love around me all the time—when I am not too busy to think!"

"That is as it should be, Joanie," Scior answered. "When our two dimensions mesh, we can do our work of guiding you and loving you so much better.

"We are still one, Joanie, even closer than we were when I was on the earth plane. And this will always be, now that we have made contact."

I know this is true. I can feel my husband's presence whenever I pause in my busy schedule and think of him.

I remember often what Peter said so many times to me, "Whatever else happens to you in your life, know that you have been LOVED."

I know it. And I know I am still loved.

* * * * *

There may be those of you who think this account is weird or scary or bordering on something evil. That it is wrong to try to make contact with those who have left the body.

One day we all make this journey, this transition. Some fear it; some welcome it; some put it from their minds and refuse to countenance it, shying away from what is a normal, natural occurrence.

How do we know that the baby in the womb does not fear the leaving of this cozy condominium to be forced into an alien world? Yet every day, babies are born and most of us greet the event with joy. Why should we not greet with joy the birth into another world? And the more knowledge we have of what is to come, the less fear and apprehension there would be.

Those we have loved and who have gone before us into this other world do not love us the less for temporarily leaving us behind. Why should we think that conversing with them by some means other than the sound vibrations in the air is odd or peculiar?

A hundred years ago if someone had talked about having a box in the house which showed pictures of things happening at that moment on the other side of the world, they would probably have been put in a mental home. Nobody would have believed them. But today we accept television as perfectly normal, even if we don't understand how it works.

Angel conversations and contacts with humans have been taking place since time immemorial. There are many accounts in the Bible of communications from this other world. Who is to say in what form they occurred? Many times we do not know. The writer does not tell us exact details.

There are natural laws with which we are still unfamiliar. Science does not have all the answers. A doctor cannot even tell you what sleep is or how it works to restore the body.

But we do not have to know the gaseous composition of the sun to enjoy its warmth and to reap its benefits. We do not have to know what makes a flower bloom in order to enjoy its perfume and beauty.

Do not, therefore, be afraid to attempt to contact someone you love who is no longer in the body. It may take time. You may have to be patient and build up the vibratory influences necessary to do this. One week of tennis lessons does not qualify you to play at Wimbledon, nor a month of piano instruction enable you to give a concert in Carnegie Hall.

As Scior said so often, meditation is the start. It is necessary to still the mind and leave time for these contacts.

Approach this slowly, with love and respect and sincerity. Do not expect instant results. Do not tell others what you are attempting to do; negative input is a great killer.

This is our secret, yours and mine.

May you be blessed in your endeavors.

**End**

Printed in the United Kingdom
by Lightning Source UK Ltd.
9853000001BB/14